*I would not for any thing in the world omit
the seeing of that renowned citie of Venice,
which of many is called the impossible
within the impossible*

[JOHN FLORIO, *Second Frutes*, 1591]

SHAUL BASSI
ALBERTO TOSO FEI

SHAKESPEARE IN VENICE

EXPLORING THE CITY WITH SHYLOCK AND OTHELLO

photographs by
GABRIELE GOMIERO

ELZEVIRO

SHAKESPEARE IN VENICE
EXPLORING THE CITY WITH SHYLOCK AND OTHELLO

Copyright © Elzeviro

First edition 2007

PIETREPARLANTI SERIES

*graphic design, coordination
and editorial direction*
Alessandro Tusset

authors
Shaul Bassi
Alberto Toso Fei

translator
John Millerchip

photographs
Gabriele Gomiero

graphic illustrations
Valter Fenuccio

printers
Centrooffset Master

EDITRICE ELZEVIRO
via A. Diaz 20, 31100 Treviso
info@elzeviro.com
www.elzeviro.com

ISBN 88-87528-19-5

I may speak of thee
as the traveller doth of Venice:
Venetia, Venetia,
Chi non ti vede, non ti pretia.

[LOVE'LABOUR LOST, atto IV scena II]

id *William Shakespeare* visit Venice, perhaps during the "lost years" between 1585 and 1592, when we know little of what he was doing and where he went, or did he only imagine the city from a distance? This book will not provide the answer, but its pages do invite the reader, whether curled up in an armchair or lost in the labyrinth of the city, to explore Shakespeare's Venice. For the *calli* and *campi* of Venice tell many stories and Shakespeare could never resist a good story. Given the simple fact that there is no evidence that he ever left England, the consensus amongst scholars is that Shakespeare never set foot in Italy, but he nevertheless set many of his plays there, from *The Merchant of Venice* and *Othello* in the *Serenissima* to *Romeo and Juliet* in Verona and *The Taming of the Shrew* in Padua.

Yet as one strolls around Venice today one sees fewer changes than in any other Renaissance city and there is a strong temptation to believe the opposite. There are so many places, so many majestic monuments and hidden corners that seem to whisper "Shakespeare was here". And in a sense we don't have to abandon the illusion, for what this book has to tell may well have reached his ears from the tales of well-travelled friends, from books and from the Venetian merchants who ate and drank at the *Oliphant Inn*.

So what we suggest is that you, dear reader, put yourself in Shakespeare's shoes: if you are perusing these pages in the comfort of your own home, then travel in your imagination, as he probably did; if you have the good fortune to be staying in Venice, use the book as a sort of guide, choosing as you will, to start at St. Mark's, the main gateway to the city, as if the young William had arrived by sea, or from the Ghetto, as if he had come overland and crossed the lagoon by "the traject, […] the common ferry/Which trades to Venice", as Portia does in *The Merchant of Venice*. Whichever approach you decide on, do not at any cost forgo the pure pleasure of getting lost and perhaps discovering other Shakespearian associations that the authors have overlooked.

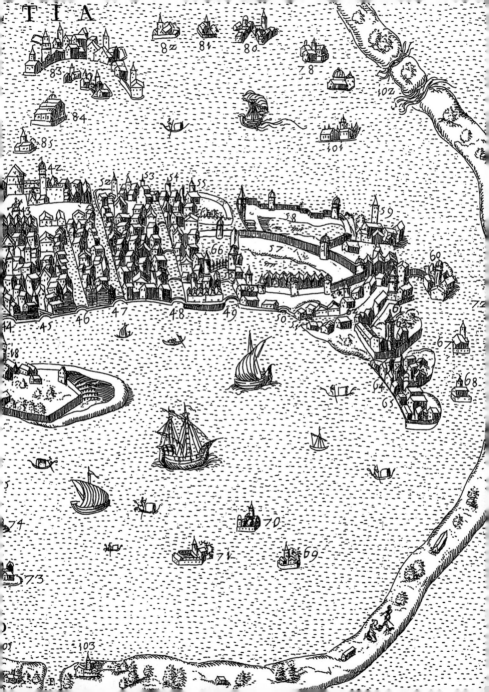

THE HUB OF POWER

PORTIA – *It must not be. There is no power in Venice*
Can alter a decree establishèd.
'Twill be recorded for a precedent,
And many an error by the same example
Will rush into the state. It cannot be.
[THE MERCHANT OF VENICE, Act IV, Scene I]

OTHELLO – *Ah balmy breath, that dost almost persuade*
Justice to break her sword!
[OTHELLO, Act V, Scene II]

TITUS – *Sir boy, let me see your archery.*
Look ye draw home enough, and 'tis there straight.
Terras Astraea reliquit.
[TITUS ANDRONICUS, Act IV, Scene I]

 [1] VENICE AS JUSTICE

    n *The Merchant of Venice* Shylock demands justice from the State for Antonio's failure to honour his side of their contract but in the end he finds himself the victim of his own intransigence. In *Othello*, the Moor takes justice into his own hands and kills his wife, Desdemona, whom he believes has been unfaithful; when he discovers that he has been deceived he condemns himself to death for the tragic error and carries out the sentence himself. During the Renaissance Justice was the virtue that Venice placed firmly at the centre of the mythical image it projected of itself and Venetian justice was celebrated as much by foreign as by Venetian historians and chroniclers. If he had ever visited St. Mark's, Shakespeare, like every other traveler, would have been dazzled by the beauty of the Doge's Palace and would certainly have noted the statue of Justice high up on the façade. The English traveler *Thomas Coryat*, who came to Venice in 1608 (so shortly after Shakespeare might have been there), writes that "*at the very highest top of all, is advanced the Image of Lady Justice with a naked sword in one hand, and a ballance in the other hand, sitting upon a couple of Lyons made of alabaster*". On the West façade there is another statue, by the sculptor *Filippo Calendario*, which depicts Venice personified as a woman, whose brandished sword again recalls the image of Justice.

To understand the spirit with which justice was administered in Venice one need do no more than translate the Latin inscription above the entrance to the Avogaria in the Doge's Palace: "*Before anything else, always investigate thoroughly in order to establish the truth with justice and clarity. Condemn no-one, except after honest and balanced judgement. Judge no-one on the basis of suspicion but seek out evidence and let the sentence be compassionate. Do not do unto others anything that you would not have done to you*".

Despite this wise counsel, Venetian history is stained with some appalling miscarriages of justice: in 1622 *Antonio Foscarini*, a nobleman who was Venetian ambassador to the Court of King James's, was executed after being convicted of "*having had secret and frequent contact with ambassadors of foreign powers* […] *both by day and by night, with and without disguise, and having revealed to them, in exchange for money, the most* […] *intimate secrets of the Republic*". The venue for these meetings was *Palazzo Mocenigo*, the residence of the English ambassador. And the assumption was that the clandestine encounters took place through the offices of the young *Anne of Shrewsbury*, Countess of Arundel.

After Foscarini's death, the Lady Arundel was advised to leave the city immediately. But far from running away Anne, who was evidently as indomitable as her godmother, *Elizabeth I*, went straight to the Doge, *Antonio Priuli*. Though we have no proof that the contemporary version of what passed between them – Anne was said to have made it clear that the sole purpose of Foscarini's night-time visits was to go to bed with her – was anything more than salacious gossip, it remains a fact that the Countess demanded and obtained a public declaration of innocence. And before she left Venice, less than six months later, Foscarini too was acknowledged to be innocent; his body was exhumed and the authorities publicly admitted their error and honoured his memory with a state funeral.

Before Foscarini, a baker's apprentice called *Piero Faccioli* had had the ill fortune to fall foul of Venetian justice, and though there are no court records to substantiate his story it is deeply rooted in the Venetian imagination. In March 1507, Faccioli was caught in *Calle de la Verona* with the sheath of a dagger in his hand, standing near the lifeless corpse of *Alvise Guoro*, a young cousin of *Clemenza Barbo*, who lived nearby. The youth had nothing whatsoever to do with the crime: he had simply tried to help a person who seemed in need, but the guards could see no further than his bloody hands. He protested his innocence but then, under torture, confessed to a murder he had never committed: he was found guilty and sentenced to be beheaded and quartered.

On 22nd March, everything was ready for the execution between the *columns of Marco and Todaro*: the young man had refused to defend himself and was just waiting for it all to be over. At that very moment a servant set out from the Barbo household for St. Mark's Square, running as fast as he could and shouting that the baker's boy was innocent: Lorenzo Barbo, Clemenza's husband, had confessed to killing Guoro in a fit of jealousy. But he arrived too late and the executioner's axe fell as he was still trying to push his way through the crowd. And no sooner had a member of the Council of Ten pronounced the ritual formula: "*Justice is done!*" than the news of Piero's innocence spread like wildfire. The following day the Doge summoned the judges and issued them with a warning that was repeated for centuries in Venetian court rooms during trials that might end with a sentence of death: "*… and always remember the poor baker's boy*".

In his two "Venetian" plays Shakespeare seems in fact to convey both the glory and the contradictions of this myth of impartial justice, on the one hand showing a law administered perversely by the State, first in favour of

Shylock and then against him, and on the other a man – Othello – who sets himself up as a dispenser of justice and brings about death and anguish.

Walking across the square, in front of the Basilica, Shakespeare might have noticed another mythological personification of justice, this time cast in bronze on one of the great Renaissance pedestals (*Alessandro Leopardi* 1505) supporting the three flagstaffs. The figure, to whom Shakespeare refers in both *Titus Andronicus* and *The First Part of King Henry VI* is *Astraea*, the daughter of Zeus and Themis and a goddess of justice.

At the end of the Golden Age she was the last of the immortals to abandon Earth in disgust at the wickedness of mankind and took up her abode among the stars, where she was transformed into the constellation Virgo, beside the scales of justice, Libra, which she holds. This is how the chronicler *Pietro Contarini* describes the Venetian Astraea: "*In front of the door there are three flags that blow in the gentle breeze. The lofty flagstaffs reach above the clouds.* [...] *The one in the middle shows three ships coming from the high seas. On the stern of the first ship one sees the golden Virgin of the Pole, who, having been exiled by the wicked world, has fixed her abode in Venetian waters*".

The bronze image would in fact have struck Shakespeare immediately because innumerable English poets and philosophers often referred to *Queen Elizabeth* herself as the Virgin Astraea. In linking London and Venice this myth reminds us of how Shakespeare probably saw in the *Serenissima* a mirror of the desire, aspirations and anxieties of his English mother country.

IAGO – *I am one, sir, that comes to tell you your daughter*
and the Moor are now making the beast with two backs.
[OTELLO, Act I, Scene I]

 ☞ [2] **IN THE LION'S MOUTH**
he tragedy of *Othello* starts with a denunciation. In the middle of the night Senator Brabantio is awakened by shouting and clamour echoing in the street outside his *palazzo*.
Someone has come to tell him – and probably to make sure that everyone else in the neighbourhood knows, such is the effect of even a scarcely raised voice in the narrow *calli* of Venice – that his daughter has eloped with a "lascivious Moor", the mercenary general Othello. In actual fact denunciations were normally made much more discreetly, either in a note called a *raccordo* in which the writer offered the State valuable information in exchange for favours or payment, or by resorting to the silent but potentially lethal *Bocca di Leone* – the Lion's Mouth. For many centuries secret accusations were placed in special wooden boxes fixed to the outside walls of *palazzi* or left in some public place or delivered by hand of a third party; but probably in the late 1500s the State instituted the *Bocche di Leone*, carved stone masks with parted jaws ready to receive the incriminating note. Shakespeare could have seen a fine specimen on the first floor of the Doges' Palace, in the *loggia* overlooking the Piazzetta. In his fascinating history of secret services and espionage in Venice, the historian *Paolo Preto* lists sixteen places around the city where one can still see these places, often in the shape of a lion's head, where informers could leave their allegations.

The keys to the receptacles were held by various magistrates. Contrary to what one might think, however, accusing someone was not such a simple matter: a law passed on 30th October 1387 ordained that unsigned denunciations left in the box of the Council of Ten were to be burned and their contents ignored. Another law of 1542 stipulated that anonymous accusations of blasphemy could be acted upon provided the allegation was supported by at least three witnesses prepared to swear that they were present when the alleged offence was committed. Although in 1602 the Venetian *Pier Maria Contarini* praised the role of secret denunciations in preserving the security of the State, for "*the only way of guarding against tyranny is to guarantee anonymity to accusers*", the practice came to be seen as a symptom of the aristocratic despotism of the Venetian regime during the century of the Enlightenment.

DENONTIE SECRETE
CONTRO CHI OCCVLTERA
GRATIE ET OFFICII.
Ó COLLVDERÁ PER
NASCONDER LA VERA
RENDITA D ESSI

When the Englishman *Charles Burney* visited Venice in the late 1700s he reported that the main *Bocca di Leone* was covered with cobwebs and had lain unused for a couple of centuries. At the same time, however, *Lorenzo Da Ponte*, Mozart's librettist, was cited in an allegation delivered through one of these *bocche*, located near the *Church of San Moisè*, on 28th May 1779. "*This despicable individual,*" said the accusation, "*seduced someone else's wife, with whom he now lives in unholy co-habitation and foul and illegitimate procreation*".

OTHELLO – *Most potent, grave, and reverend signiors,*
My very noble and approved good masters,
That I have ta'en away this old man's daughter,
It is most true, true I have married her.
The very head and front of my offending
Hath this extent, no more. Rude am I in my speech
And little blessed with the soft phrase of peace,
For since these arms of mine had seven years' pith
Till now some nine moons wasted, they have used
Their dearest action in the tented field,
And little of this great world can I speak
More than pertains to feats of broil and battle.
And therefore little shall I grace my cause
In speaking for myself. Yet, by your gracious patience,
I will a round unvarnished tale deliver
Of my whole course of love, what drugs, what charms,
What conjuration and what mighty magic–
For such proceeding I am charged withal–
I won his daughter.
[OTHELLO, Act I, Scene III]

IAGO – *With as little a web as this will I ensnare as*
great a fly as Cassio
[…]
So will I turn her virtue into pitch
And out of her own goodness make the net
That shall enmesh them all.
[OTHELLO, Act II, Scene I]

[3] THE DOGE'S PALACE

f Shakespeare had ever entered the Doge's Palace, he would have found himself inside one of the most imposing examples of civic architecture in Europe, the centre of Venetian power and a powerful symphony of mythological and religious symbols. A visitor at that time would have been able to admire not only centuries-old styles and decorations but also brand new works commissioned after the fire that had seriously damaged the building in 1574. It is these magnificent rooms that provide the imagined setting in which Antonio and Shylock, Othello and Brabantio appear before the Doge and the Venetian Senate.

There are so many artistic treasures in every corner of the place that it is impossible to give a detailed description or imagine the impact they might have had on the English visitor. We can, however, try to visualize him pausing at certain points as the decorative scheme works its magic.

For every work of art in the palace was intended to convey a specific message by means of the rich and complex symbology of the Renaissance. Many paintings celebrated the greatness of Venice directly, through imposing portraits of doges and magistrates and scenes of military victories and diplomatic triumphs; others achieved the same effect through allegorical figures, each understood as having very precise political meanings.

The *Sala delle Quattro Porte*, named after its four splendid doors framed with precious eastern marbles, is one of the few rooms in the Doge's Palace that has conserved its original structure (dating from the late XVI – early XVII century) substantially intact. The room performed a dual function – as an antechamber and a communicating area – and the sculptural group above each door referred to the room to which it leads.

Let's imagine that Shakespeare has stopped to look at the *Porta dell'Anticollegio*, through which all diplomatic missions had to pass to the waiting room before being received by the Doge. Here three statues by *Alessandro Vittoria* intimate the virtues the ambassadors must display if they are to encounter the favour of Doge. The moon, together with a snake and the caduceus, the sparrowhawk and wings and the cockerel with winged eyes represent the political virtues of *Eloquence, Fluency* of speech and *Vigilance*. Before pleading his case, Othello would have studied them carefully.

In defending himself against Brabantio's impassioned accusations, Othello describes himself as a rough soldier devoid of great oratory skills; in actual fact he comes out with one of the most eloquent, sophisticated and captivating speeches Shakespeare ever put in a character's mouth. It is not surprising that the Doge downplays Brabantio's charge and applauds Othello's persuasiveness with appreciative irony: "*I think this tale would win my daughter too*".

But though the Moor shows himself to be a champion in eloquence and fluency of speech, his vigilance is found wanting. Othello would have done well to note a small painting in the next room, the *Sala del Collegio*. It was here that the Doge, with his "cabinet" of *savii* or sage councillors, the Heads of the Council of Ten and the Grand Chancellor constituted one of the supreme bodies of the Republic; the Collegio received foreign ambassadors and envoys and discussed the most important questions of State. The chamber contained a superb array of canvases painted by *Paolo Veronese* between 1576 and 1578. The biggest of these were the central panels of the ceiling, depicting *Mars and Neptune, Venice Triumphant*, with *Justice and Peace*, and *Faith and Religion*, while above the throne is the allegorical *Doge Sebastiano Venier*, with *Agostino Barbarigo*, offering thanks to Christ for victory at Lepanto.

The battle itself is scarcely more than hinted at in the background, a sort of pretext for a new and important celebration of the military glories of Venice and her role as a bastion of Christianity against the infidel. But if Othello had looked up at the smaller panels in the ceiling he would have seen a series of graceful female figures embodying the virtues, one of them a young woman weaving a web. The painting may depict an allegory of *Industry* or *Dialectic* but one's thoughts are drawn immediately to the close net of falsehoods and suspicions with which the diabolical Iago eventually traps Othello.

CASSIO – *This very night, at one another's heels,*
And many of the consuls, raised and met,
Are at the duke's already.
[OTHELLO, Act I, Scene II]

DESDEMONA – *Most gracious duke,*
To my unfolding lend your prosperous ear;
And let me find a charter in your voice,
To assist my simpleness.
[OTHELLO, Act I, Scene III]

DOGE – *That thou shalt see the difference of our spirit,*
I pardon thee thy life before thou ask it.
For half thy wealth, it is Antonio's,
The other half comes to the general state,
Which humbleness may drive unto a fine.
[THE MERCHANT OF VENICE, Act IV, Scene I]

 ✍ [4] **MEETING THE DOGE**

ccording to the Myth of Venice, the city was the epitome of good government, the perfect blend of Aristotle's three types: monarchy, aristocracy and democracy.

Emblematic of this mixed system was the election of the Doge, who is depicted in both *The Merchant of Venice* and in *Othello* as the Duke and ruler of the city but also as an attentive listener to the petitions of the citizens and as guarantor of a judicial system that was equal for all, even for the Doge himself. The voting system was anything but straightforward: the several hundred members of the *Great Council* were summoned (except for those under thirty) and the ballot box was filled with small balls (called *ballotte*), one for each of the members present; thirty of the balls were gilded. Each member was summoned in turn and handed the ball extracted for him by the *balotin del doxe*, a boy chosen at random in St. Mark's Basilica by the youngest councillor and one of the Heads of the *Quarantia* (once he turned fifteen, the *balotin* was guaranteed a job in the chancellery and a place at court throughout the Doge's reign). The first electoral college comprised the thirty councillors who were handed a gilded ball and each time this happened all the other members of the recipient's family had to leave the chamber so that the thirty represented as many different families. Nine golden balls and twenty silver were now placed in the ballot box; the nine who drew the golden balls had to nominate forty electors; the same process was used to reduce these to twelve, who in turn had to elect twenty-five. Twice more the ballot box was used: to reduce the twenty-five to nine, who elected forty-five, who were reduced to eleven, who nominated the final electoral college of forty-one, whose votes actually produced the Doge (and from 1553, the forty-one electors had to be approved, one by one, by the Great Council). Once the election process was complete, the new Doge was presented to the people with the words: "*Questo xe missier lo Doxe, se ve piaxe*" (This is the Doge, if he pleases you).

Though the Italian term *ballottaggio* (a second, run-off election) entered the language from French, it actually arrived in France from Venice and its electoral system with the *ballotte*. And the English "ballot" and "ballot box" clearly had the same origin. There is even a faint reminiscence of the Venetian system in the method used to elect the President of the United States. When the former colonies of the Crown declared their independence in 1776 they sent representatives to one of the few places in the world where they elected their Head of State: the *Serenissima*. According to the *Oxford English Dictionary*, the first use of the English term "ballot" ("*A small ball used for secret voting; hence, by extension, a ticket, paper, etc. so used*") occurs in the description of Venice given by *William Thomas* in his *Historie of Italie* (1549).

Although there are several rooms in the Doge's Palace where the Doge performed various official functions we can imagine that the scenes in which he appears in Shakespeare's plays took place in the *Senate Chamber*, with its magnificent decorative scheme comprising works by *Jacopo Tintoretto, Titian, Jacopo Palma il Giovane* and *Andrea Vicentino*. An explosion of colour and late-Renaissance taste, set off by gilded frames and woodwork and the splendid official dress of the senators, a setting that still evokes echoes of the debate and discussion that preceded the main decisions. Or perhaps we should imagine the decisions on how to conduct the war with the Turks and how best to defend Cyprus being taken by the Doge in consultation with the Council of Ten.

The *Consiglio dei Dieci* was set up in 1310 in order to punish the nobleman *Bajamonte Tiepolo* and his fellow-plotters and to ensure that State security would never again be breached. It was a political tribunal par excellence; shrouded in mystery and conducting its affairs in total secrecy the Council was the custodian of the peace and prosperity of the State. As power was concentrated in the hands of an increasingly restricted number of families, the Council of Ten tended gradually to take on more responsibilities and acquired greater authority and influence, to the point where it almost became the real governing body of the State.

GRATIANO – *In christening shalt thou have two godfathers.*
Had I been judge, thou shouldst have had ten more,
To bring thee to the gallows, not to the font.
[THE MERCHANT OF VENICE, Act IV, Scene I]

LODOVICO – *For this slave,*
If there be any cunning cruelty
That can torment him much and hold him long,
It shall be his. You shall close prisoner rest
Till that the nature of your fault be known
To the Venetian state.
[OTHELLO, Act V, Scene II]

 [5] DEATH AND TORTURE IN THE PIAZZA
During the Renaissance, torture and the death penalty were common practice; they were exemplary punishments carried out in full public view. Shakespeare frequently alludes to them in his work, and the two Venetian plays are no exception. Shylock saves himself from them by accepting forced conversion but they certainly await Iago on the island of Cyprus, and Ludovico makes it clear that his punishment will be bloody and merciless.

The English traveller *Thomas Coryat* offers a contemporary description of the places reserved for executions: "*At the South corner of St. Markes Church as you go into the Dukes Palace there is a very remarkable thing to be observed. A certaine Porphyrie stone of some yard and halfe or almost two yards high, and of a pretty large compasse, even as much as a man can claspe at twice with both his armes. On this stone are laide for the space of three dayes and three nights, the heads of all such as being enemies or traitors to the State [...] In that place do their heads remain so long, though the smell of them doth breede a very offensive and contagious annoyance.* [...] *Near to this stone is another memorable thing to be observed. A marvailous faire paire of gallowes made of alabaster, the pillars being wrought with many curious borders and workes, which served for no other purpose but to hang the Duke whensoever he shall happen to commit any treason against the State. And for that cause it is erected before the very gate of his Palace to put him in minde to be faithfull and true to his country, if not, he seeth the place of punishment at hand. But this is not a perfect gallowes, because there are only two pillars without a transverse beame, which, beame (they say) is to be erected when there is any execution, not else. Betwixt this gallowes malefactors and condemned men (that are to goe to be executed upon a scaffold betwixt the two famous pillars* [...] *at the South end of St. Marks street, neare the Adriaticque Sea) are wont to say their prayers to the Image of the Virgin Mary, standing on a part of S. Marks Church right opposite unto them."*

Coryat states that the two alabaster pillars near the *Porta della Carta* were used to hang any Doge found guilty of high treason. In fact he was probably the credulous victim of some contemporary wiseacre, for the history of the *Serenissima* offers no evidence to support the theory. What they do commemorate is a victory the Venetians scored over the Genoese at Acre in 1256.

Another occasional place of execution, still in the Piazzetta, was between the two pink marble columns of the *loggia Foscara* of the Doge's Palace, the ninth and tenth in line from the ceremonial entrance of the *Porta della Carta*.

One tradition has it that it was from here that the Doge witnessed the executions, another that this was the spot from which the laws of the *Serenissima* were proclaimed. A documented example of their use for capital punishment is that of *Bartolammeo Memmo*, who was hanged between the two columns on 14th July 1470 for having conspired against Doge *Cristoforo Moro*: "*Vegnimo diese a consegio domenega che vien* – the "Annals" of *Domenico Malipiero* quote the very words he was alleged to have used – *et le corazzine sotto la veste, e amazemoli, comenzando da questo becco de Cristoforo Moro*" (we'll be present at the Great Council meeting at 10 o'clock next Sunday, with breastplates under our clothes, and we'll slaughter them, starting with that cuckold Cristoforo Moro). The first to have the dubious honour of being hanged between the two red columns, however, was *Girolamo Valaressa*, seven years earlier on 23rd November 1463.

Those condemned to death were comforted and accompanied to the scaffold by the members of the two confraternities that together formed the *Scuola di San Fantin*, which met in the building that now houses the *Ateneo Veneto*,

---

On 6th July 1480, three Jews from Portobuffolè, a small town under Venetian jurisdiction near Treviso, were burned alive between the columns of the Piazzetta after being judged guilty of killing a Christian child to use his blood for ritual purposes. This episode is the only known example in Venetian history of "blood libel", the phenomenon that spread across Europe after the case of *William of Norwich*, in England in 1141.

The legend of the Jew drinking Christian blood (which curiously overlaps with Protestant objections to Catholic ritual during Communion) might also underlie the penalty of the pound of Antonio's flesh that Shylock insists on inserting in their contract. The writer *Caryl Phillips* recounted the Portobuffolè episode as part of his novel *The Nature of Blood* (1997), interweaving it with the story of Othello, told through the eyes of the Moor.

just opposite the opera house *La Fenice*; they were known as the Guild of the "Good Death". The commonest methods of execution in Venice were hanging and beheading, preceded by the cutting off of one or both hands in particularly heinous cases and often followed by the quartering of the offender, the four parts being displayed as a warning in the four parts of the city. Then there was another, especially brutal means of executing prisoners: by bludgeoning them to death. The chronicles give several accounts of this violent and harrowing practice, which in at least one case was inflicted on a woman, Bernardina, who was convicted of murdering her husband in 1521. In his entry for 3rd August that year the diarist *Marin Sanudo* recounts that her right hand was hacked off at the site of the crime; then, with her severed hand hanging from her neck, she was carried by barge along the Grand Canal to St. Mark's, where she was clubbed to death before being drawn and quartered. Sanudo decribes Bernardina's atrociously long-drawn-out agony and his shock at the gruesome display of the quartered corpse of the first woman to suffer such a punishment.

Turning for a moment from history to legend, we must mention the fourth column from the corner of the ground floor arcade on the lagoon side of the Doges' Palace, which offered condemned prisoners a last chance of reprieve before they climbed onto the scaffold: bare-footed, facing inwards and with their hands tied behind their back, they had to try and edge around the outer face of the column without stepping off the low marble base. The marble is very worn… but there is no record of anyone managing to perform the feat.

BISHOP OF CARLISLE – *Many a time hath banished Norfolk fought*
For Jesu Christ in glorious Christian field,
Streaming the ensign of the Christian cross
Against black pagans, Turks, and Saracens;
And toiled with works of war, retired himself
To Italy, and there at Venice gave
His body to that pleasant country's earth,
And his pure soul unto his captain, Christ,
Under whose colours he had fought so long.
[RICHARD II, Act IV, Scene 1]

EMILIA – *I know a lady in Venice would have walked*
Barefoot to Palestine for a touch of his nether lip.
[OTHELLO, Act IV, Scene III]

 ☞ [6] **"BANISHED NORFOLK" AND THE PLAGUE**

he passing mention of *Norfolk – Thomas de Mowbray*, first Duke of Norfolk (1366 – 1399) – is an important link in relations between Shakespeare and Venice for it was the search for traces of Norfolk in 1833 that first engaged the energies of *Rawdon Brown*, who later invented many stories of presumed Venetian models for Othello. Mowbray was exiled and stripped of his title by *Richard II* in 1398, after the king fell-out with *Henry Bolingbroke*, the future *Henry IV*, over suspicions that they were both involved in the conspiracy against the *Duke of Gloucester*.

He travelled to Venice, intending to proceed to the Holy Land, but died there of the plague on 22nd September 1399. The story of Norfolk brings to mind two very important aspects of Venice's history: its role as an embarkation point for the final stage of journeys towards Palestine (ironically recalled by Emilia in *Othello*) and the tremendous impact that various plague epidemics had on the city.

In accordance with his instructions, Norfolk's body was repatriated in 1533 but his tombstone remained in Venice, where Shakespeare could have seen it set into the façade of the Doge's Palace that looks out over the water towards the Island of San Giorgio (the patron saint of England, as the historian *John Julius Norwich* noted). *Rawdon Brown* passed on the story that the stone was removed by Napoleon's soldiers in 1810, when they recognized the insignia of one of the hated English enemy. Brown saw the arms reproduced in the book *The merits of the Venetian Nobility, sketched through the arms of each family* written by the Frenchman *Casimir Freschot* in 1682, where they are mistakenly attributed to a Venetian family. His attention was drawn by several common English heraldic symbols, including the "*Lion and Cap of maintenance*" of the Mowbrays and the white deer of *Richard II*.

The story slips into the realms of legend when Brown relates that he had the idea, one Christmas Day, of showing the book to an elderly mason who had done some work for him. Not only did *Domenico Spira* recognize the stone but he turned out to be the only Venetian who knew what had happened to it because it was he who had been engaged by the French invaders to remove it from the façade and to chisel away the carving so that it could be used as a paving slab. But Spira, at great risk to his life, devised a ploy to circumvent his instructions: he smoothed down the "wrong" side and hid the sculpted

Rawdon Brown (1806-1883), an English gentleman and Oxford graduate, moved to Venice where he stayed for over half a century and became the city's most illustrious foreign resident and a point of reference for all English vistors, including his close friend *John Ruskin*. For over twenty years he worked in the Venetian archives to produce the monumental *Calendar of State Papers and Manuscripts relating to*

English Affairs existing in the Archives of Venice and Northern Italy (six volumes published between 1864 and 1886); the unfinished work was taken up by the Scots man *Horatio Brown*.

A chapter is devoted to the two (unrelated) Browns in *Paradise of Cities* by *John Julius Norwich*, which relates how the eccentric Rawdon concocted various legends linking Shakespeare and Venice.

surface face downwards. To his great surprise therefore, Brown was eventually able to admire the tombstone whose whereabouts had so intrigued him in the workshop of a Venetian stonemason.

The next step was to smuggle the heavy slab on board an English ship once a plaster cast had hurriedly been made. Norfolk's tombstone can now be seen at *Corby Castle* in southern Cumbria, the home of the *Howard* family, descendants of Mowbray.

SOLANIO – *I should be still*
Plucking the grass to know where sits the wind,
Peering in maps for ports and piers and roads.
[THE MERCHANT OF VENICE, Act I, Scene I]

PROSPERO – *Me, poor man – my library*
Was dukedom large enough.
[THE TEMPEST, Act I, Scene I]

 [7] SHAKESPEARE IN THE LIBRARY

ne only needs to glance at the eight volumes of *Geoffrey Bullough's Narrative and Dramatic Sources of Shakespeare* to realize that Shakespeare was an extremely curious, voracious reader despite the fact that, unlike the other poets and playwrights of his time, whom he consistently overshadowed (and who in turn were often noisily envious), he had no formal university education and had, in *Ben Jonson's* famous words, "*smalle latine and lesse greeke*".

Most of Shakespeare's works were not entirely original: indeed, Shakespeare was an extraordinary "inventor" in the sense classical rhetoric attributed to the term: *inventio* did not involve creation from nothing but rather the selection of the most suitable material from an existing classical repertory. In St. Mark's Square Shakespeare would certainly have been attracted by the *Marciana Library*, the temple of Renaissance culture, born from the bequest of the great poet *Francesco Petrarca*, whose sonnets provided the model for those of Shakespeare and many other English poets such as *Thomas Wyatt* and *Philip Sidney*. In his description of the Library, the traveller *Thomas Coryat* also mentions statues that have now disappeared which depicted personalities who were dear to Shakespeare.

"*It happened that when I was very diligently survaying these antiquities, and*

*writing out inscriptions, there came a youth unto me, who because he thought
I was a great admirer and curious observer of auncient monuments, very courte-
ously brought me into a faire chamber, which was the next roome to Cardinall
Bessarions Library, so famous for auncient manuscripts both Greeke and Latin,
where I observed a little world of memorable antiquities made in Alabaster
[…] Julius Caesar in alabaster, but little more then his head: Cleopatra in
alabaster, onely her head with a blacke vaile about it. The same againe with
stumpes without any hands, and her serpent by her, with which she stung her
selfe to death: Pompey the Great, a little more then his head: Augustus Caesar
at length in alabaster with a long gowne or mantle about him: Marcus Anto-
nius the Triumvir in alabaster to the middle […] This Library did first belong
to Francis Petrarcha, who by his last will and testament made the Senate of
Venice heire thereof".*

The Library is also the right place to pose a question to which historians have
still not been able to give a satisfactory answer: did Shakespeare speak Italian?
Though many of his sources were unquestionably Italian, it is thought that for
the most part he read them in English or French translations. The Library still
has a 1559 edition of *Il Pecorone* by *Ser Giovanni Fiorentino* (which served as
the basis for the novella which in turn provided Shakespeare with the main
plot of *The Merchant of Venice*) and various XVI century editions of the
Hecatommithi by *Giambattista Giraldi Cinzio*, the collection from which came
the *novella* that inspired Shakespeare to write *Othello*.

Venice was certainly one of the greatest producers of books in the whole of
Europe at the time. Printers set up shop in the *Serenissima* within a few years
of *Johann Gutenberg*'s invention of movable type in Mainz around 1440.
Among them was *Giovanni Da Spira*, who was granted a special licence in
1468. Even before him, the printer-priest *Clemente da Padova* was active in
the city. And 1468 also marks the date of the first book to be printed in
Venice, *Cicero*'s *Epistolae*.

Perhaps the most famous of all Venetian printers was *Aldo Manuzio*, who was also the first to use the "*italic*" style (commissioned from *Francesco Griffo* of Bologna in 1501), the elegantly sloping version of the roman type then popular. Manuzio was also credited with being the first to popularize pocket-size books in octavo format, starting with *Il canzoniere del Petrarca*, published between the end of the XV and the beginning of the XVI century.

But Venetian printers did not confine their attentions to books in Italian or Latin: the first edition of the *Koran* to be printed with movable type was published in Venice in 1530, and in 1520-23 the first *Talmud*, the paging of which is still based on the first Venetian versions.

ALDVS · PIVS · MANVTIVS · R.

Venice built a reputation as a leading producer of maps and sea-charts (like those mentioned by Solanio in *The Merchant of Venice*) as well as literary works. One of the most famous cosmographers in Venetian history was *Fra Mauro*, who died at a venerable age in 1459, in the *monastery of San Michele in Isola*, where he had a kind of cartographic workshop. Generally considered the finest example of late-mediaeval map-making, a globe created by him is now conserved in the *Marciana Library*, and other exceptional works include a cosmographic chart commissioned directly by *King Alfonso V of Portugal*, and a magnificent map which is now in the Vatican Library in Rome.

Fra Mauro never travelled: he traced his maps by following the minutely detailed information provided by Venetian seafarers.

One day, as he was working on his planisphere, *Fra Mauro* received a visit from a group of noblemen together with a Senator of the Republic. They began to ask more or less relevant questions about geography, except for the senator, who could manage no more than spluttering dismissal: "*What is this paper, this drawing? It looks like scribbles!*" Calmly, the priest explained that what the patrician could see were the countries of the world, with their mountains, rivers, seas and cities. "*How enormous the world is,*" mused the Senator, and then he asked where Venice was. "*This dot here is Venice,*" replied the priest, pointing to a spot on the map. The nobleman was incensed and looking at the friar he said: "*Well make the world smaller and Venice bigger!*". And off he went.

OTHELLO – *O my fair warrior!*
[…] Come, Desdemona.—
Once more, well met at Cyprus.
[OTHELLO, Act II, Scene I]

MARDIAN – *Not in deed, madam, for I can do nothing*
But what indeed is honest to be done.
Yet have I fierce affections, and think
What Venus did with Mars.
[ANTONY AND CLEOPATRA, Act I, Scene V]

 ✦☞ [8] VENICE AS VENUS
The Othello scholar E.A.J. Honigmann expressed his surprise
that in a tragedy set for the most part in Cyprus, "no-one
mentions Venus!", for according to legend the goddess of love
and beauty was born from the waves of the sea off Paphos in the south west
of the island. Perhaps Shakespeare wanted specifically to avoid placing too
much emphasis on a series of associations that would have been very sug-
gestive for his more cultivated contemporaries. Venus was linked not only
with Cyprus but also with Venice, an identification encouraged but their
similar-sounding names. Though *Francesco Sansovino's Venetia città nobilissima et singolare* (1581) imaginatively suggests that the name Venezia derives
from the Latin "*Veni etiam*" (come again, return) and the Englishman
Thomas Coryat asserted in 1611 that "*the worde is altered from the auncient
name by the addition of the letter v; for the olde name was Enetia, which came
from the word Eneti a people of Paphlagonia*", other contemporaries preferred
to trace its origins to Venus: "*Aut Venus à Venetis sibi fecit amabile nomen, /
Aut Veneti Veneris nomen, et omen habent*" (an anonymous poet quoted in
Giovanni Nicolò Doglione's Venetia trionfante et sempre libera, 1613).

Like Venus, Venice was born from the waves and, according to legend, the birth date was 25th March 421, when Venus was in the ascendant.

Shakespeare could have admired a carved figure of Venus, which was also a symbol of Venice's dominion over Cyprus, in the panel on the right of the *Loggetta* by *Jacopo Sansovino*, at the base of the bell tower in St. Mark's Square. Cyprus became part of the Venetian Empire in 1489, when *Caterina Cornaro*, the Venetian who had been queen of the island since 1472 following her marriage to *James II of Lusignano*, ceded her realm to the *Serenissima* in exchange for the seigneury of Asolo in the province of Treviso. Her story became emblematic of the complex power games then being played for control over the Eastern Mediterranean. She was widowed shortly after her marriage and legend has it that her infant child and heir to the throne was poisoned by the Venetians in order to ensure their control of the island. But Cyprus remained a Venetian colony only until 1573, when it was reconquered by the Ottoman Empire immediately after the legendary *Battle of Lepanto* (1571) in which Venice and the other European powers defeated the Turks. When *Othello* was first produced in the early 1600s therefore, the audience knew that Cyprus as a Venetian possession was already a thing of the past.

In the politics of appropriation of classical divinities which, as the historian *David Rosand* explains in his *Myths of Venice*, was something Venice systematically practised in the 1500s, the ideal partners for Venus were Neptune and Mars, whose colossal statues stand at the top of the *Giants' Staircase* in the courtyard of the Doge's Palace. It is very interesting that Othello and Desdemona can be identified in various ways with the god of war and the goddess of love. When the Moor refers to "*my fair warrior*" or when Iago sneeringly comments that "*Our general's wife / is now the general*", the image of Desdemona comes close to that of the *Venus Victrix*, the conqueror of men's hearts or the victorious contestant in the Judgement of Paris.

It is even more interesting that the paradoxical pairing of Venus and Mars had a special significance for Renaissance philosophy and politics. According to myth, the daughter of the two divinities was Harmony, who inherited the contrasting qualities of her parents, the martial spirit of her father and her mother's beauty and tenderness, and gave rise to the maxim *Harmonia est discordia concors* (or the more classical *concordia discors*).

Harmony, at a time of bloody wars of religion in Europe, had become a symbol of peace and concord between nations. In Shakespeare's tragedy the paradoxical couple of Othello and Desdemona miraculously escape war with the Turks and win a brief period of harmonious peace, only for it to be quickly undermined by an envious enemy who significantly describes their love in terms of a harmony he is determined to destroy: "*O, you are well tuned now: but I'll set down / the pegs that make this music*" [Act II Scene I].

DESDEMONA – *That I did love the Moor to live with him*
My downright violence and storm of fortunes
May trumpet to the world.
[OTHELLO, Act I, Scene III]

OTHELLO – *...alas, to make me*
The fixed figure for the time of scorn
To point his slow unmoving finger at!
[OTHELLO, Act IV, Scene II]

RODERIGO – *What a full fortune does the thicklips owe*
If he can carry't thus!
[OTELLO, Act I, Scene I]

 [9] ST. MARK'S: A GALLERY OF "MORI"

thello, says the title of the tragedy, is "the Moor of Venice".
In the principal source of the work, the novella by *Giambattista Giraldi Cinzio, Gli Hecatommithi*, Shakespeare had read:
"*There once lived in Venice a Moor, who was very valiant and of a handsome person; and having given proofs in war of great skill and prudence, he was highly esteemed by the Signoria of the Republic, who in rewarding deeds of valor advanced the interests of the state.*" But what exactly is meant by "a Moor"?
The only certainty is that for centuries the critics have engaged in heated debate about an identity which in many ways is mysterious and blurred and on which the text never throws clear light, for Renaissance knowledge fused reality and imagination into what has been defined as "poetic geography" when it came to countries outside Europe, and in Africa in particular.
Let's suppose that Shakespeare has just read Cinzio's novella in the *Biblioteca Marciana* and decides now to ask a passerby where he can find the Moors

(*i mori*) of Venice. Curiously, he doesn't have to leave St. Mark's Square to find at least four kinds, each very different from the other. The most famous and easiest to see are the great bronze statues that strike the hours at the top of the *Clock Tower*, built by *Mauro Codussi* between 1496 and 1499.

These powerful male figures, cast in 1497 by *Ambrogio da le Anchore*, are clad in animal skins that leave them half naked. A contemporary document, a note detailing the expenses entailed in the construction of the building, refers to the two figures as *Ziganti* (giants) but there is no certainty as to who they were intended to depict, though they were probably biblical or mythological references to an earlier age. But before long, probably as a result of the dark brown colour of the bronze or the patina that formed on the surface, the Venetians took to calling them "Moors" and the clock tower is still known as the "*Torre dei Mori*".

Looking up at the tower from the Square, the traveller of four centuries ago would have seen what nowadays we can admire only twice a year, during the week following *Ascension Day* (in Venetian dialect *Sensa*) and on the Feast of *Epiphany*: from one of the two doors at the sides of the dial, where normally we see the hours and minutes, the The Three Magi emerge in procession and, preceded by the Angel, bow before the Virgin as they pass. One of the Magi, the dark-skinned king *Balthasar*, may be the "*fixed figure for the time of scorn / To point his slow unmoving finger at*" that Othello fears he will become.

If you move now towards the corner between the Basilica and the Doge's Palace, you will see the unsettling and enigmatic group of the *Tetrarchs*, four figures of warriors embracing each other, sculpted in Egypt in the IV century from a single block of porphyry. They depict the Emperor *Diocletian* and the other members of the tetrarchy; the hole visible in the headdress of each was once set with the symbol of their royalty. Venetians prefer to believe that the sculptures are none other than four Saracens (or Moors) who were turned to stone as they tried to steal the Treasure of St. Mark's.

Support for this attractive theory might be deduced from the crude, late XIII century sculpted frieze below; this depicts two *putti* emerging from the mouths of two dragons bearing a cartouche inscribed with one of the earliest examples of vernacular language in Venice: "*L'om po far e die in pensar – E vega quelo che gli po inchontrar*" (which loosely translates as: "Men will do and say whatever they feel like – and then they'll learn the consequences"). It would seem like a classic case of projection for it was well known that the theft was perpetrated by Venetians just as it was Venetians who stole the body of St. Mark from Alexandria by concealing it under a layer of pork, which was repugnant to the Moslem guards.

And lastly, on the XIV century *capital of the Peoples of the Earth*, the third from the left on the water side façade, we can see the proud turbaned head of a Moor, complete with the thick lips Rodrigo insultingly refers to when speaking of Othello.

This gallery of Moors actually within the Square shows how the term could be used in many different and inventive ways and became almost a generic word for "otherness", applicable both to recognizable ethnic physiognomies and to creatures shrouded in legend. When we move towards *Campo dei Mori* in the *Sestiere* of *Cannaregio*, things will get more complicated.

DUKE – *Tis certain then for Cyprus. Marcus Luccicos, is not he in town?*
I SENATOR – *He's now in Florence.*
DUKE – *Write from us to him; post-post-haste, dispatch.*
I SENATOR – *Here comes Brabantio and the valiant Moor.*
DUKE – *Valiant Othello, we must straight employ you*
Against the general enemy Ottoman.
[OTHELLO, Act I, Scene III]

 [10] MEN OF ARMS: BARTOLOMEO COLLEONI
he Turks are moving to attack Cyprus and Venice must send its fleet to defend its possession. It is often forgotten that the Doge and Senators think first of a Florentine general to lead their forces, but he is not available so their choice falls on Othello, the Moorish general who had "rendered services to the State" on a previous occasion. In *De magistratibus et republica venetorum*, the book by *Gasparo Contarini* that Shakespeare almost certainly read in an English translation, it says that "*...some forrain men and strangers haue been adopted into this number of citizens, eyther in regard of their great nobility, or that they had beene dutifull towardes the state, or els had done vnto them some notable seruice* [...] *the Captaine Generall of our Armie* [...] *is alwaies a stranger*". The tradition was, in fact, that no Venetian-born citizen should gain any political advantage from military success. One of the most famous "forrain men" (which in this case meant soldiers from other Italian states) to have fought under the banner of St. Mark was the *condottiero* or mercenary general *Bartolomeo Colleoni*, whose equestrian statue stands in *campo SS. Giovanni e Paolo* and is considered one of the absolute masterpieces of Renaissance sculpture. The statue, by *Andrea Verrocchio*, was paid for from a bequest that Colleoni himself left orders to be paid into the coffers of the Serenissima on condition that an equestrian monument be erected to him in *St. Mark's Square*.

Personality cults were forbidden under the Republic, however, and by long tradition not even a Doge was allowed to have a statue of himself in the Square.
But a State that was short of funds was never going to accept the loss of tens
of thousands of ducats without a struggle, so a compromise was found.
As he had wished, Bartolomeo Colleoni got his statue in front of St. Mark's.
Not in St. Mark's Square though, but in the space before the Scuola Grande
di San Marco, the headquarters of the *Guild of St. Mark*, beside the *Church
of Santi Giovanni e Paolo*...
Andrea Verrocchio never finished the statue: in a fit of pique prompted by
the news that the commission to cast the rider might be given to *Bellano da
Padova*, he smashed the plaster cast of the horse (with which he had started
the work). Sentenced to death because of this insult to the Republic, Verrocchio fled to Mantua, but before long he was pardoned, having apologized
to the Serinissima and arguing that without his own head he would not be
able to remake (much better) the head of the horse that he had destroyed.
In actual fact, Verrocchio only cast the statue of Colleoni; after his death the
casting of the horse was entrusted to *Alessandro Leopardi* (the creator of the
three great bronze flagpole bases in St. Mark's Square) but he accepted the
commission with some misgivings because Verrocchio had designated one
of his disciples to complete the work. In any case, from then on the sculptor became universally known as Alessandro *"dal Cavallo"* ("of the horse"),
and the place where he lived and worked is still called the *corte del Cavallo*.
Relations between the Serenissima and its *condottieri* were not always idyllic.
On one side of the Basilica of St. Mark's there is a large porphyry head that
is popularly known as "the head of Carmagnola" (though a sculpture with
different features but the same name can be seen over the door of the bell-
tower at San Polo). *Francesco Bussone*, better known as *Carmagnola*, was a
daring and ambitious *condottiero* who entered the service of the Venetian
Republic after the breakdown of his relations with *Filippo Maria Visconti*.
Suspected of having betrayed the Venetians in the wars against the Duke
of Milan (though victorious at the *Battle of Maclodio*, he inexplicably

allowed thousands of enemy soldiers to flee) he was tricked into returning to Venice and promptly imprisoned; after being held for three days without food "*he was bound in preparation for torture; first they broke an arm, then they hauled him clear of the ground and dropped him, and finally they applied fire to the soles of his feet. The confession he made was carefully transcribed*".
After 29 days in prison he was beheaded on 5th May 1432 and his last home in the city, *Palazzo Lion*, on the Grand Canal near the *Church of San Stae*, was razed to the ground.

The debate over the innocence of Carmagnola continues to rage and his story was retold by the celebrated XIX century writer *Alessandro Manzoni* in the tragedy *Il Conte di Carmagnola*, in which general is portrayed as a loyal servant of the Republic who is sacrificed for reason of state.

Whatever the truth, it remains a fact that as Francesco Bussone's fortunes were plunging a young soldier was beginning to cover himself with glory on the field of battle: and his name was *Bartolomeo Colleoni*.

Niccolò Machiavelli, the most important political thinker of the Italian Renaissance, was convinced that Venice's use of mercenary soldiers was a disastrous mistake; he maintained that the Venetians were defeated at the historic *Battle of Agnadello* in 1509 because their mercenaries were effeminate, luxury-loving and idle and lacked the boldness and courage even to defend themselves.

KING HARRY – *Follow your spirit, and upon this charge*
Cry, 'God for Harry! England, and Saint George!'
[HENRY V, Act I, Scene III]

BASTARD – *Saint George, that swinged the dragon, and e'er since*
Sits on's horseback at mine hostess' door,
Teach us some fence!
[KING JOHN, Act II, Scene I]

 ☙ [11] "SAINT GEORGE THAT SWINGED THE DRAGON"
ravellers love to go in search of new experiences but not
infrequently, the very fact of being far from home drives
them to seek out something familiar; perhaps the more so in
a city like Venice, which astonishes and bewilders the visitor at every turn.
Arriving at St. Mark's, Shakespeare would have seen the *island of San Giorgio*
Maggiore, just across the water, and he wouldn't have had to walk far to reach
another place dedicated to the patron saint of England, the Christian hero
who saved a princess from a dragon – St. George.
As his biographer, *James Shapiro*, notes, Shakespeare was born on 23rd April,
St. George's Day (or perhaps the day before), in a town, *Stratford-upon-Avon*,
that was especially devoted to the saint. But when he was a child the
Protestant Reformation ensured that all sacred images were removed from
sight, including those of St. George, the last of which was taken out of the
stained glass windows of the Guild Chapel in Church Street in 1571, when
Shakespeare was seven years old.
It's reasonable to suppose, therefore, that if he had had the chance he would
certainly have been attracted by a cycle of paintings dedicated to the deeds
of St. George adorning the walls of the *Scuola Dalmata dei Santi Giorgio e*
Trifone, otherwise known as the *Scuola di San Giorgio degli Schiavoni*, which,

as a guild chapel, might have been easier to enter than a Catholic church (unless, of course, we accept the theory of some scholars that Shakespeare was a closet-Catholic, as his father had probably been).

It was the flourishing community of Dalmatians (known in Venice as "*Schiavoni*" or Slavs) that commissioned *Vittore Carpaccio* to decorate their *Scuola* and we can well imagine Shakespeare standing before the most famous of the canvases, *The Duel of St. George and the Dragon* (1504-07). Just as Shakespeare liked to do, so Carpaccio drew on an ancient source, the mediaeval best-seller, the *Golden Legend* by *Jacopo da Varagine* and "modernized" the story by weaving sacred and profane themes from XVI century Venice into it. So the English visitor would have found himself before a scene that was at once familiar and exotic.

Unquestionably familiar, the story of the Christian knight who killed the dragon outside the Libyan city of *Silene* and saved the princess who was about to be sacrificed to the monstrous creature that demanded to be fed a virgin from the city every day. As a sign of gratitude the king, who had sought in vain to save his daughter, agreed to convert to Christianity, along with all his people.

In Venice the term "*Scuola*" was used to denote a meeting place used by a Confraternity devoted to a particular saint or by a Congregation or Guild of people who practised the same trade or craft or who practised the same trade or craft or who were linked by their place of origin; the group would meet not only to pray but also to provide mutual help and support or to organize charitable activities. There were dozens of them scattered around the city, but only six had the right to call themselves "*Scuola Grande*".

But the setting in which Carpaccio places his narrative of the final duel is decidedly disconcerting. As the art historian *Augusto Gentili* notes, the side of St. George and the princess features a Western, Christian landscape with the positive connotations of Mediterranean vegetation, a hermitage on the hillside and two ships. The side of the dragon, with its urban landscape of palm trees, towers and minarets, fuses East and West, paradoxically rather like Venice, with its hybrid architecture.

The Christian knight who defends the beautiful damsel from the lecherous demon; the stories of conversion and battle on African soil; the naked, dismembered corpses of the dragon's latest victims, offering a ghoulish close-up of sex and death; the lizards and the toads, hellish creatures that populate the corrupted imagination of Othello; the horizon with one ship sailing before the wind and the other drifting, as in the minds of Antonio and Shylock in *The Merchant of Venice*; a city that like Venice is an amalgam of Rome, Jerusalem and Byzantium, Jews, Christians and Moslems: all are themes that Shakespeare dramatized in his peerless fashion in the two plays set in Venice.

LORENZO – *How sweet the moonlight sleeps upon this bank!*
Here will we sit, and let the sounds of music
Creep in our ears. Soft stillness and the night
Become the touches of sweet harmony.
Sit, Jessica; Look how the floor of heaven
Is thick inlaid with patens of bright gold.
There's not the smallest orb which thou behold'st
But in his motion like an angel sings,
Still choiring to the young-eyed cherubins.
Such harmony is in immortal souls,
But whilst this muddy vesture of decay
Doth grossly close it in, we cannot hear it.
[THE MERCHANT OF VENICE, Act V, Scene I]

 [12] SHAKESPEARE AND THE KABBALA

ccording to one of the most fanciful and tempting theories regarding Shakespeare's intellectual nourishment, he was interested in *Kabbala*, the ancient mystical and speculative current in Jewish thought. *Kabbala*, a word that in Hebrew means simply "tradition", reached Venice at the same time as the newly established Jewish community and in particular thanks to the Jews expelled from Spain, with its rich history of mystical meditation. *Kabbala* possesses keys capable of reconciling the different modes in which science and religion interpret creation and life. *Kabbala* teaches science humility and respect for mystery; it teaches the importance of developing all aspects of human beings, not only of logical reasoning and the satisfaction of physical needs. During the Renaissance interest in *Kabbala* spread to Christians (the most famous was *Pico della Mirandola*), and many believed it could perfectly well be incorporated into their religion. In Venice, for example, the friar *Francesco Giorgi* (or *Zorzi* in Venetian), like all Christian adepts in *Kabbala*, was convinced that it fore-shadowed the Second Coming of Christ. Fusing Jewish, Christian and neo-Platonic elements in a perfect example of Renaissance intellectual synthesis, *Fra Giorgio* wrote *De harmonia mundi*, whose theories of harmonizing the macrocosm and the microcosm found artistic application in the construction of the *Church of San Francesco della Vigna*, which the Kabbalist friar planned according to "harmonic" calculations. Giorgi was also consulted by two emissaries sent by *Henry VIII*, who was collecting opinions as to the divorce he was contemplating (see also the chapter devoted to *Leon Modena*), and his teachings exerted a considerable influence in the Elizabethan period on thinkers such as *John Dee* and *Robert Fludd*.

In his important work *The Occult Philosophy in the Elizabethan Age* the celebrated scholar *Frances Yates* suggests that Giorgio also influenced Shakespeare. Commenting on the somewhat reckless theories of *Daniel Banes*, who saw the characters of *The Merchant of Venice* as embodiments of the *Sefiroth*, the ten emanations of the divine – with Shylock in the part of the "*Ghevurah*" or "judgement-severity", Antonio as "*Hesed*" or "loving kindness" and Portia

---

Not far from the site where the *Church of San Francesco della Vigna* now stands (it took its name from the biggest and oldest vineyard in Venice) there was, until 1810, a small church dedicated to St. Mark. According to tradition, it was here that the Evangelist happened to be blown ashore during a storm, while he was preaching the Gospel in these parts. And here too that the saint had the vision of the angel who pronounced the famous words: "*Pax tibi Marce evangelista meus!*" (Peace be unto you, Mark, my evangelist!), which in

later centuries became the motto of the city. Let's move now – magically! – to the other side of Venice, to the *Church of the Madonna della Salute*, the construction of which is based on an erudite play on numbers which is half Jewish and half Christian. Nearby there is a canalside path called *fondamenta de Ca' Bala'*, and scholars hotly debate whether or not there was ever a Bala' family that might have given its name to the thoroughfare. If not, here more than in other places the name "cabala" would arouse exciting associations.

as "*Tifereth*" or "beauty or mercy", who reconciles the first two (Banes uses this interpretation to show that the play was not an enactment of the conflicting positions of Jewish law and Christian charity but rather an exploration of Kabbalistic synthesis) – Yates takes a more cautious approach and writes of the famous dialogue between Lorenzo and Jessica: "*we may therefore suppose that the immediate inspiration for this outburst was the universal harmony of the Friar of Venice*". He goes on to suggest that Shakespeare's play is not anti-Semitic in spirit but an invitation to tolerance. And in this connection we should also remember (as mentioned in the chapter devoted to Venus and her birth) that in Othello too, music and harmony are important elements.

Other scholars have been very sceptical of the idea of an esoteric Shakespeare. Responding to *Frances Yates*, who had described the expression on Shakespeare's face in his funeral bust in Stratford as "trance-like", *William Empson* commented that the expression more probably indicated the effects of a "*city banquet, with a series of grand courses and a round of wines*" which the poet found it difficult to keep down.

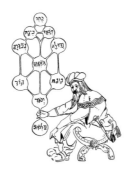

THIRD GENTLEMAN – *A noble ship of Venice*
Hath seen a grievous wrack and sufferance
On most part of their fleet.
[…] *The ship is here put in,*
A Veronessa…
[OTHELLO, Act II, Scene I]

SALARINO – *Your mind is tossing on the ocean;*
There, where your argosies with portly sail,
Like signiors and rich burghers on the flood,
Or, as it were, the pageants of the sea,
Do overpeer the petty traffickers,
That curtsy to them, do them reverence,
As they fly by them with their woven wings.
[…] *My wind cooling my broth*
Would blow me to an ague when I thought
What harm a wind too great might do at sea.
I should not see the sandy hour-glass run
But I should think of shallows and of flats,
And see my wealthy Andrew docked in sand,
Vailing her high-top lower than her ribs
To kiss her burial. Should I go to church
And see the holy edifice of stone
And not bethink me straight of dangerous rocks,
Which touching but my gentle vessel's side
Would scatter all her spices on the stream,
Enrobe the roaring waters with my silks,
And in a word, but even now worth this,
And now worth nothing?
[THE MERCHANT OF VENICE, Act I, Scene I]

[13] THE ARSENALE: VENICE'S POWERHOUSE

enice's real power base lay in its control of the sea, and its ships were the source of its wealth. In *Othello* it is warships that dominate, avoiding battle with the Turkish fleet thanks to a providential storm, while merchant ships are the key to events in *The Merchant of Venice*, bringing both fortune and disaster to the characters in the play. Curiously, Shakespeare makes specific mention of two kinds of vessel that do not seem to have been amongst the main craft that sailed under the flag of St. Mark. As the expert on boats in the Veneto region, *Gilberto Penzo*, explains, the "veronessa" cited in *Othello* probably refers to a heavy barge with inward curving mast tips used on the River Adige (which runs through Verona), though it has also been suggested that Shakespeare was alluding to the fact that Venice kept part of its fleet on standby in the rivers of the area. And as regards the "argosies" mentioned at the beginning of *The Merchant of Venice*, the vessels in question in fact belonged to the merchant fleet of the *Republic of Ragusa* (present-day Dubrovnik), which remained proudly independent of Venice despite their close trading links. *Frederic Lane*, the foremost economic historian of Venice, reminds us that Shakespeare could actually have seen *ragusee* on the Thames. But more than that, Shakespeare might well have seen – if not had first hand acquaintance with, if we accept the often voiced theory that his detailed knowledge of naval matters could only have come from direct experience as a sailor – various Venetian ships, most of which had been built in the legendary *Arsenale*, the biggest dockyard in Europe. The great *Dante Alighieri* (1265-1321), who visited Venice several times and saw the Arsenale in its heyday, immortalized it in *Canto XXI* of the *Inferno*: "*As, in the Venetian arsenal, the clammy tar / Is boiled in winter to caulk the damaged ships / When they can't be navigated as things are, / So they're rebuilt instead, and, on the slips, / One plugs the ribs of those much travel-worn; / Some make new oars, or twist ropes in their grips; / Some hammer at the prow; some stern that's torn, / While others mend the jib, another one / Repairs the mainsail where*

it has been shorn" (Translation by *Peter Dale*, Anvil Press, London, 1996).
The great gateway into the Arsenale, built in 1460 when *Pasquale Malipiero*
was Doge, was transformed into a commemorative monument following
Sebastiano Venier's naval victory over the Turks at the *Battle of Lepanto* in 1571.
Also dating from this period are the two winged victories and the statue of
Santa Giustina on the pediment. The terrace, with its eight allegorical statues,
was added a hundred years later. The lions on either side of the terrace tell a
different story. The two biggest were sent back by *Francesco Morosini* as spoils
of war following his re-conquest of the Morea (the Peloponnese) in 1687.
The name *Arsenale* is a corruption of the Arabic "*dar sin'ah*", two words meaning "house" and "manufacture". Founded, according to tradition, in 1104, the
shipyard provided work for over sixteen thousand "*arsenalotti*" within its high
crenellated walls when operating at full stretch; and the chronicles relate that
they could assemble a fully fitted warship in the space of just twelve hours.
In the last years of the 1500s, a hundred were launched in just two months
and such was the fame of Venice's Arsenale that the word was adopted by
fourteen languages. During Henri III's state visit in 1574, a galley was built,
rigged and provisioned during a reception in the French king's honour, and
he can hardly have failed to be impressed by this deliberate demonstration of
Venice's power and organizational skill in case of attack or other contingency.

The observations of Salerio at the beginning of *The Merchant of Venice*, which show us how he and his fellow merchants Antonio and Solanio are so obsessed by the outcome of their trading enterprises that they see ships literally everywhere, may provide an eloquent psychological touch but they are nonetheless historically inaccurate. Venetian merchants and nobles (often the same person) did indeed love to see vessels constantly around them, as we know from the inventories of their houses that often included ornaments, vases, carafes, jewels, spice-boxes and other objects in the form of ships; and their tables often bore *spongade*, a sort of fruit cake sometimes shaped like a boat; but these were evidence of pride and prosperity not of anxiety. It obviously served the story to have Antonio unable to repay his debt to Shylock because his argosies were reported to have foundered, but cargoes were normally covered against loss and Venice was one of the leading centres of maritime insurance.

Dockyard workers in Venice, the *arsenalotti*, were held in such high regard by the city's hierarchy that they were the only people, other than members of the nobility, who were not obliged to kneel in the presence of the Doge, and they were considered as his personal bodyguard. Something of this dual link between St. Mark's and the *Arsenale* must have survived to modern times: the Fire Brigade, normally stationed in the Arsenale, have the honour of presiding over the hoisting and lowering of the three great flags in St. Mark's Square. And it was in these two places that the celebrated revolt against the Austrian occupation began under the leadership of *Daniele Manin* and *Niccolò Tommaseo* in 1848.

DON PEDRO – *Nay, if Cupid have not spent all his quiver in*
Venice thou wilt quake for this shortly.
[MUCH ADO ABOUT NOTHING, Act I, Scene I]

Two households, both alike in dignity
In fair Verona, where we lay our scene,
From ancient grudge break to new mutiny,
Where civil blood makes civil hands unclean.
From forth the fatal loins of these two foes
A pair of star-crossed lovers take their life
Whose misadventured piteous overthrows
Doth with their death bury their parents' strife.
[ROMEO AND JULIET, Prologue]

 [14] A VENETIAN ROMEO AND JULIET
very year thousands of people troop to *Via Cappello* in Verona,
to gaze at the balcony that brought together Romeo and Juliet,
the most famous young lovers in the world. As usual, Shakespeare drew on various sources; the most direct was the long poem by *Arthur
Brooke* entitled *The Tragical History of Romeus and Juliet* (1562), which drew
in turn on authors such as *Matteo Bandello* and *Masuccio Salernitano*. It
would appear, however, that the story that originally inspired the Italian
writers in fact took place in Venice and culminated in the *Church of San
Pietro di Castello*, which stands in the only *campo* in Venice still to be covered with grass – a beautiful spot which is sadly neglected by tourists.
The protagonists of this story were called Elena Candiano and Gerardo Guoro.
They too were young and of noble birth, but unlike their Veronese counter-
parts Elena and Gerardo grew up together in a peaceful environment with
friendly relations between their respective families. The couple's friendship

eventually turned to love and they married secretly with the help of the woman who had nursed them both and without telling their parents.

So frightened were they that their families might have different ideas as to their future and might forbid their union that they continued to live apart, even after they had married, and to wait for the right moment to reveal the truth. Of course the young couple had plenty of opportunities to meet since their families had been on excellent terms for many years.

One day Gerardo's father sent him to the East, as happened to many Venetian youngsters, to help with the family's trading interests in the Levant. But during his absence, Candiano obliged his daughter to accept a proposal of marriage from his fellow nobleman Vittore Belegno. Elena did not know what to do; Gerardo was far away and she could not make public admission of a situation that would have made her father a laughing stock and cast dishonour on her family for ever.

With fear and anguish clutching at her heart, Elena went into a deep faint, to the point where she was believed to be dead, and was buried in the Church of San Pietro di Castello. On that very day, her husband returned home, unaware of what had happened. In despair, when he learnt of what had befallen Elena, he freely confessed to the secret marriage, for no parental punishment could mean anything beside the loss of his beloved.

Then, before anyone could stop him, Gerardo ran to the church, removed the stone slab covering his wife's tomb and collapsed, weeping uncontrollably, over Elena's body. Then the miracle: the tears and kisses of her husband revived Elena and, unlike Romeo and Juliet and with the forgiveness and blessing of their parents, the Venetian lovers lived happily ever after.

OTELLO – *I do beseech you,*
Send for the lady to the Sagittary,
And let her speak of me before her father.
[OTHELLO, Act I, Scene III]

☞ [15] **IN THE SIGN OF SAGITTARIUS**

hen Brabantio accuses him before the Doge of having "stolen" Desdemona, Othello pleads that his bride be allowed to speak for herself. Twice Shakespeare's text names "the Sagittary" as the place where Desdemona lives and many commentators have glossed it as the name of an inn. Others have preferred to dig a little further, remembering how Shakespeare loved to charge even the smallest details in his works with hidden meaning. In this case, they suggest associations with the mythological figure of the centaur, the hybrid creature depicted as drawing a bow in the sign of the zodiacal constellation Sagittarius, which recalls both the anomalous union of Othello and Desdemona and the "*beast with two backs*" which Iago obscenely evokes to enrage Brabantio (see the chapter on the *Bocca di Leone*). But the explanation could in fact be something a good deal simpler and more direct. The Sagittary might in other words refer to the place in Venice where arrows (in Latin *sagittae*) were made and sold; this was the *Frezzeria* or *Frezzaria*, which is still a busy shop-lined *calle* leading to St. Mark's Square. The Venetian historian *Sabellico* called this street "*vicus sagittarius*".

Laws were passed in the 1300s that obliged all Venetians between the ages of 16 and 35 to practise crossbow shooting on the beach at the Lido once a week. Later, the advent of firearms made the practice obsolete. Also in the "*Frezzeria*", under the sign of the "Sun", was the workshop of *Giacomo Franco*, the celebrated copper engraver who lived in Venice between 1550 and 1620 and produced the often reprinted illustrations of Venetian costumes collected in *Habiti d'huomeni et donne venetiane.*

RODERIGO – *Here is her father's house, I'll call aloud.* [...]
IAGO – *Awake, what ho, Brabantio! thieves, thieves, thieves!*
Look to your house, your daughter, and your bags.
Thieves, thieves! [...]
BRABANTIO – *What tell'st thou me of robbing? This is Venice.*
My house is not a grange.
[OTHELLO, Act I, Scene I]

 [16] THE HOUSE OF DESDEMONA

As mentioned in the chapter dealing with secret accusations, Othello opens with Iago and Roderigo engaged in noisy wrangling beneath the window of the Senator Brabantio. One tradition accredited in many guidebooks, identifies the place as *Palazzo Contarini-Fasan*, a small jewel of florid Gothic architecture on the Grand Canal, of which *John Ruskin* executed a fine watercolour. It was certainly common practice for Venetian families to attach their name to the building where they lived and even the most imposing *palazzi* are still known, with a not entirely convincing show of modesty, as *Ca'* (the abbreviation of casa or house/home). So it is difficult to fathom why, probably in the XIX century, a building that belonged to a branch of the illustrious Contarini family that was renowned for its pheasant shooting should suddenly have become "*Ca' Brabanzio*".

The main access into Venetian *palazzi* was the water entrance from the canal and the labyrinthine approach to *Ca' Contarini-Fasan* on the land side makes it difficult to imagine the spot from which Iago and Roderigo could have yelled their insinuating insults to the elderly nobleman in an example of *charivari*, the ancient ritual whereby a community publicly stigmatized unconventional marriages, deviant conduct and offences against ethical and moral standards with shouting and loud discordant music. Perhaps the most logical answer is that the *palazzo* is near St. Mark's and stands on a route used by gondoliers, who are notoriously prone to inventing stories to satisfy the appetites of Shakespeare-loving English and American tourists; indeed, as *John Pemble* makes clear in his *Venice Rediscovered*, gondoliers made an enormous contribution, after the fall of the Republic and throughout the XIX century, to the creation of a second – this time romantic and crepuscular – myth of Venice.

But there is one small detail that gives rise to another alluring line of thought. The elegant fretted balconies praised by Ruskin feature a wheel pattern, careful examination of which reveals that one of these wheels is "turning" in the opposite direction to all the others. Think now of the ancient image of the wheel of fortune, the symbol of uncertainty and of the folly of pride, which Shakespeare describes as a blindfolded goddess *"depicted with a wheel to signify – this is the point – that she is turning and inconstant, and all about change and variation"* [*Henry V*, Act III, Scene VI]. So perhaps we can imagine that the balcony wheels offer an allusion to the tragic fate of Desdemona, the imaginary inhabitant of the *palazzo*, whom fortune first destines for overwhelming, passionate love and then nullifies it through her cruel and tragic death.

SHYLOCK – *What, are there masques? Hear you me, Jessica,*
Lock up my doors; and when you hear the drum
And the vile squealing of the wry-necked fife,
Clamber not you up to the casements then,
Nor thrust your head into the public street
To gaze on Christian fools with varnished faces,
But stop my house's ears—I mean my casements.
Let not the sound of shallow fopp'ry enter
My sober house.
[THE MERCHANT OF VENICE, Act II, Scene V]

 [17] SHAKESPEARE AT THE "FANCY-DRESS PARADE"
hakespeare was fascinated by masks and disguises of all kinds. Many of his plots revolve around characters who conceal or change their identity, as, for example, does Portia in *The Merchant of Venice* when she presents herself as a legal expert in order to save Antonio. And it is no coincidence that one of the poet's favourite books was *Ovid's Metamorphoses*. So we can surely take it for granted that if he ever did come to Venice, Shakespeare would have been attracted by the theatrical and festive atmosphere of Carnival. Masks and fancy dress could be worn in Venice from October until Shrove Tuesday, although the Carnival season really took off from the *Feast of St. Stephen* or *Boxing Day*, when a sort of parade called the "*Liston delle Maschere*" launched the city into weeks of excess.

The roots of the impulse to dress up, to indulge in drinking and revelling reach far back in time and any number of theories purport to identify the origins of the modern Carnival: there are those who trace it back to the ancient Roman festival of Saturnalia, others to Dionysian orgies, and still others to long-lost Chaldean rituals. Whatever the truth, mask- and costume-wearing has always had a ritual significance: it involved being able to shuffle off one's public identity and being free to follow one's instincts in a strange fusion of truth and illusion; a sort of magic costume that conferred a new and unexpected power on anyone who wore it. In actual fact, this presumed omnipotence was pure illusion: donning a mask may have generated an impression of being able to cast off the constraints and ties of one's everyday life; but in reality it wasn't like that, as *Giustiniana Wynne de Rosenberg* perceptively notes in a letter addressed to her brother: "*the costume was the* maschera veneziana, *which you know well and which may be called a camouflage of convention rather than decoration. Its use is as much a boon to the common people as to the nobility. For a large part of the year it conceals you and gives a wonderful feeling of freedom. People believe that since when they look like gentlefolk they do in a certain sense become like gentlefolk. In its wisdom, the Government has granted special privileges concerning masquerading and the lower classes, poor fools, feeling flattered by this sensitive tutelage of common interests, believe that no-one is any longer of a higher rank when they have a mask to cover their face*".

Promenading was a must during Carnival and amongst the most famous was that of *Campo Santo Stefano*, where the paraders strolled up and down a strip of stone paving laid across the centre of the square, the rest of which was grassed, like the other Venetian *campi* (incidentally, the paved strip was called a *lista*, hence the term for a promenade, *liston*). There is an engraving by *Giacomo Franco*, which shows "*people in mask and costume in Venice during Carnival,* [...] *who almost all congregate in Campo S. Stefano at 11 pm and stay there, strolling up and down until almost 2 o'clock in the morning*". It was in *Campo Santo Stefano*, too, that the last *bull-baiting* entertainment to take place in Carnival was held on 22nd February 1802. This was a sort of *corrida* (bears were sometimes used instead of bulls) that was a feature of the latter part of Carnival, together with simpler events such as wheelbarrow races.

All the festivities in general – especially private events organized by and for the nobility – always had an aura of dazzling display. Amongst the most popular of masked disguises was the *Bautta*, comprising a *tricorn* hat, a shoulder-length veil and a white mask (*larva*), which the upper classes took particular advantage of to move incognito around the city. This anonymity was not always a guarantee of advantage however, as an espisode of 1548 shows: after enjoying the jousting and tilting in *Campo Santo Stefano* in the company of a bishop and an abbot, the *Duke of Ferrandina* went on to Murano for another festivity. His identity concealed behind his mask, he started to flirt with a local gentlewoman and aroused the anger of *Marco Giustinian* and another Venetian nobleman. In the ensuing brawl Giustinian struck a mortal blow at the head of the Duke, who in turn, by mistake, managed to stab his friend *Fantino Diedo*: both died within a few days.

Though Shylock derided the "shallow fopp'ry" of the Christians' masquing, which enabled them to carry off his daughter Jessica, it is also true he would shortly be taking part in *Purim*, a form of Jewish carnival that celebrates the Hebrews' deliverance from massacre planned for them by the evil Persian minister Haman, as told in the Book of *Esther*. We have precise information about how *Purim* was celebrated in the Venetian Ghetto and the historian *Brian Pullan* tells the story of a young Christian sailor, *Giorgio Moretto,* accused by the Inquisition of failing to observe the abstinence of Lent by celebrating *Purim* along with the Jews. Moretto's defence was to state that he had wished to court a Jewess, Rachel, the daughter of Isaac "the Deaf Man", who, like Shylock, locked up his doors and stopped his house's ears. Moretto's submission was not believed and he was given a light sentence. But he was unable to keep away and when he was again caught in the Ghetto he was sentenced to three years in the galleys; "*So this Lorenzo*", writes Pullan, "*never managed to elope with his Jessica*".

Campo Santo Stefano has a curious connection with England. In 1585 a thunderbolt struck the bell tower of the church and fused the bells. These were replaced by four bells from England, where the Reformation had wrought havoc with bells and bell towers: so a piece of the English Catholic tradition, so important for Shakespeare's family, had found its way to the heart of Venice, though during Carnival the divine peal now had to compete with the pealing laughter of merrymakers.

ROSALINE – *Another of these students at that time*
Was there with him, if I have heard a truth.
Biron they call him, but a merrier man,
Within the limit of becoming mirth,
I never spent an hour's talk withal.
His eye begets occasion for his wit,
For every object that the one doth catch
The other turns to a mirth-moving jest,
Which his fair tongue, conceit's expositor,
Delivers in such apt and gracious words
That agèd ears play truant at his tales
And younger hearings are quite ravishèd,
So sweet and voluble is his discourse.
[LOVE'S LABOUR'S LOST, Act II, Scene I]

HOLOFERNES – *The preyful princess pierced and prick'd a pretty pleasing pricket;*
Some say a sore; but not a sore, till now made sore with shooting.
The dogs did yell: put L to sore, then sorel jumps from thicket;
Or pricket sore, or else sorel; the people fall a-hooting.
If sore be sore, then L to sore makes fifty sores one sorel.
Of one sore I an hundred make by adding but one more L.
[LOVE'S LABOUR'S LOST, Act IV, Scene II]

 ﹏ [18] THE SELECT CIRCLES OF THE ERUDITE
n a still relevant, albeit mysterious book, written at the time
of Shakespeare but not published, because of its explosive
contents, until the mid-1800s, the philosopher *Jean Bodin,*
one of the founders of modern political philosophy, wrote: "*We arrived in*
Venice, the common haven of almost all peoples, if not of the whole world, not

*only because Venetians love to see and play host to others but also because one can
live here in perfect freedom; and while the threat of civil wars, tyrannical rulers,
harsh taxes and tiresome interference in one's personal affairs hangs over all other
cities and regions, I would say that this city alone seems immune to all these
forms of slavery"*. Although the opening words of the *Colloquium of the Seven
about Secrets of the Sublime* are perhaps over-optimistic with regard to freedom
of expression (as we shall see in the next chapter, about *Palazzo Mocenigo*),
there is no doubt that Venice was the freest of all the great cities of Europe,
Catholic but independent of Rome and hospitable to religious minorities.
Though some scholars doubt that it was actually by Bodin, this seven-sided
dialogue about religious tolerance certainly reflects the kind of discussions
that went on in places like the *Ridotto* on the mezzanine floor of *Palazzo
Morosini* on the Grand Canal (now known as *Palazzo Contarini dei Cavalli*
because of the rearing horses that decorate its façade).
Meeting places such as the *Ridotto Morosini* brought together laymen and
religious figures, Venetians and "foreigners", and any man of science or
letters who might be passing through the city. Here they were able to
engage in civilized, informal conversation about any subject, though literary and philosophical topics were most common. Amongst the famous
participants in discussions at the ridotto created and led by *Andrea
Morosini*, an official historian of the Venetian Republic and a leading
member of the so-called "young" party that opposed the more conservative group of "the old men" of Venetian politics, were *Galileo Galilei*,
Paolo Sarpi (to whom the last chapter of this book is dedicated) and
Giordano Bruno (whom we shall be speaking of in a few pages).
If scholars are right in believing that Shakespeare was actively involved
in his contemporaries' debates about the burning issues of religion, politics and philosophy, he would certainly have found his way to
academies such as the *Ridotto Morosini* if he had visited Venice.
In particular, some have seen a similar setting recreated in *Love's Labour's Lost*
the strangest of Shakespeare's comedies and rich in sophisticated plays on

words, subtle and abstruse allusions, enigmas and erudite terms (including the longest word the poet ever used, "*Honorificabilitudinitatibus*").

Not only does the play include a character called *Biron* (in some versions *Berowne*), who has been associated with *Giordano Bruno* since the XIX century, but also a baffling riddle that the scholar *Gilberto Sacerdoti* has unravelled to see an invitation to *Queen Elizabeth I* (who saw the play presented at Court) to exercise "self-sovereignty", to assume absolute political and religious power in a way that no lay-person had done since the fall of the Roman Empire, in order to limit the pernicious consequences of the recent wars of religion that had left Europe weakened and bloodstained.

That Venice was a hub of throbbing intel-lectual activity can also be deduced from a plaque set into the left wall of *Ca' Loredan* (now, with the adjoining *Ca' Farsetti*, Venice's City Hall). The inscription notes that this was the birthplace of *Elena Lucrezia Corner Piscopia*, the first woman graduate in the world, who was awarded her doctorate at the University of Padua in 1678 with a dissertation on *Aristotle*.

Shy and modest, Elena died at the age of 38; she knew Greek, Latin, Hebrew, French, Spanish and Italian; she studied music and mathematics; and she had a thorough grasp of dialectics, philosophy, theology and astronomy.

CLEOPATRA – *If it be love indeed, tell me how much.*
ANTONY – *There's beggary in the love that can be reckoned.*
CLEOPATRA – *I'll set a bourn how far to be beloved.*
ANTONY – *Then must thou needs find out new heaven, new earth.*
[ANTONY AND CLEOPATRA, Act I, Scene I]

 👉 [19] **THE PERILS OF PALAZZO MOCENIGO**
n the previous chapter we hinted at possible connections between Shakespeare and *Giordano Bruno,* who spent some years in London and between 1584 and 1585 published there his most important works in Italian, such as *La cena delle ceneri* and *Gli eroici furori,* the latter dedicated to the poet *Sir Philip Sidney.* The Italian philospher had an extremely troubled career and on his travels all over Europe he aroused lively interest amongst cultured individuals and monarchs (we know, for instance, that *Elizabeth I* owned an elegant, leather-bound edition of his *Italian dialogues*), but his revolutionary ideas also encountered incomprehension and derision in more conservative intellectual circles such as the University of Oxford.

And it was precisely because of this climate of hostility, if not of outright persecution, that many Renaissance intellectuals learned the delicate art of dissimulation, of concealing compromising ideas behind apparently innocuous, sometimes very affected, language. So it shouldn't surprise us that reading between the lines of the amorous dialogue that opens *Antony and Cleopatra* reveals the presence of a precise allusion to the most devastatingly unsettling of the theories *Giordano Bruno* developed in England. When Antony professes boundless love for the Egyptian queen and she imagines the need to set limits to the space it occupies, he responds with the image of a new heaven and a new earth which, echoing the famous words of the *Apocalypse,* alludes to the universe of infinite worlds theorized by Bruno.

Going beyond even *Copernicus*, who imagined a universe that was no longer geo-centric but still confined within the sphere marked by the fixed stars, Bruno foreglimpsed the discoveries of modern cosmology, and Shakespeare, as shown by various scholars, was fully responsive to the insights, together with a number of other English literary figures such as *Walter Raleigh*, *John Florio* and *Thomas Digges*.

By the time Shakespeare wrote *Antony and Cleopatra*, the trajectory of Bruno's life and career had already plunged to its tragic end. After various wanderings, he reached Venice, in the hope that he might be appointed to the chair of mathematics at the prestigious University of Padua. Indeed he taught there for three months and in 1592 he was in nearby Venice as the guest of the nobleman *Giovanni Mocenigo*, who was so struck by the experience of reading one of Bruno's works that he appointed him to teach him the *art of memory*. But after only two months of residence in the sumptuous *Ca' Mocenigo Vecchia*, a XV century *palazzo* near *San Samuele*, his ambitious but frustrated host – a man of mediocre intellectual gifts and not of the calibre to be able to take part in discussions at the Ridotto Morosini – saw no improvement in his memory despite his talented guest's best efforts so had the philosopher imprisoned in the *palazzo* on the 22nd May and denounced him to the Inquisition. Mocenigo reported that he had denied the divinity of Christ, the virginity of Mary and the Holy Trinity; he had practised the art of divination and had proclaimed himself a better magician than Christ, who was merely a seducer of the masses; he had stated that "*the world is eternal, that there is an infinite number of worlds and that God is continually making others*". Such statements were in fact over-simplifications of ideas that Bruno had professed for years, but in this case the famously tolerant Venice, so fiercely independent of the Papacy, decided to extradite the heretic to Rome and handed him over to the tribunal of the Holy Office. After eight years of retractions and half-recantations, trials and tortures, Giordano Bruno was burned at the stake in *Piazza Campo dei Fiori* in Rome (where today there is a statue in his memory) on 17th February, 1600.

Ca' Mocenigo Vecchia is said to be still haunted by the philosopher's ghost. So terrible was Bruno's agonizing death that every year, on the anniversary of his execution, the friar's ghost returns and makes his presence felt through paranormal phenomena connected with water, the one element that could have extinguished the flames of the fire that killed him so hideously: water pipes will suddenly burst, taps inexplicably turn themselves on, screws come loose, floods rise. Sometimes, over the centuries, the spectre of the philosopher friar has actually appeared in person but it remains a mystery as to why the only witnesses have been women... and not young women either, for Giordano Bruno only appears to those of over eighty-five years of age. Decidedly less paranormal but still strange is the fact that on the four hundredth anniversary of the execution, a plaque in memory of the philosopher was unveiled on the façade of the palazzo... and within a short time it had disappeared. The memory of Giordano Bruno still disturbs Venice.

The most celebrated tenant of the double *palazzo* of *Ca' Mocenigo Nuova* and *Ca' Mocenigo Vecchia* was *Lord George Gordon Byron*, who stayed there in 1818.
His exploits in Venice have become the stuff of legend: his wild gallops along the Lido, the lessons in Armenian on the Island of San Lazzaro, the exhausting swims along the Grand Canal, all ways of trying to dispel his persistent romantic melancholy.

Between these walls Byron wrote *Beppo*, a part of the tragedy *Marino Faliero, Sardanapalus, The Vision of Judgement* and the first cantos of *Don Juan*, doubtless inspired by his own adventures, including the tempestuous Venetian affair with *Margarita Cogni*, the "baker's girl", who at a certain moment flew at him with a knife before throwing herself from the window into the waters of the Grand Canal.

THE MARKET OF THE WORLD

SHYLOCK – *Now, what news on the Rialto?*
[THE MERCHANT OF VENICE, Act I, Scene III]

SHYLOCK – *Signor Antonio, many a time and oft*
In the Rialto you have rated me
About my moneys and my usances
Still have I borne it with a patient shrug,
For sufferance is the badge of all our tribe.
You call me misbeliever, cut-throat dog,
And spit upon my Jewish gaberdine,
And all for use of that which is mine own.
Well then, it now appears you need my help.
[THE MERCHANT OF VENICE, Act I, Scene III]

SHYLOCK – *There I have another bad match: a bankrupt,*
a prodigal, who dare scarce show his head on the Rialto;
a beggar, that was used to come so smug upon the mart.
[THE MERCHANT OF VENICE, Act III, Scene I]

PETRUCHIO – *Give me thy hand, Kate. I will unto Venice,*
To buy apparel 'gainst the wedding-day.
[THE TAMING OF THE SHREW, Atto II, Scena I]

 ☞ [20] **BUSINESS IS BUSINESS**
ialto is the only place in Venice that Shakespeare mentions
– and repeatedly – in his work. *Rialto* was the name of one of
the earliest settlements on the islands that comprise the city
(its name, from the Latin *Rivus Altus*, which later became *Rivoalti*, indicates
an island whose high shores made it possible to build without being hindered

by the tide) and it subsequently developed into the pulsating heart of Venetian trade and finance. According to legend it was here, on 25th March, 421, with the founding of the small *Church of San Giacometto*, that Venice was born; and here too, in 809, that Doge *Angelo Partecipazio* moved the seat of administrative and commercial power from *Metamauco*, which had become dangerously vulnerable to attack by Charlemagne's son *Pipin*. And it is here that Antonio insults and spits on Shylock before he needs his loan, and here that he feels ashamed to return to when he can no longer repay the debt.

At the time of Shakespeare the market area had already been completely rebuilt after the terrible fire of 1514, which had razed most of the district to the ground. The arcades of the *Fabbriche Vecchie* and the *Fabbriche Nuove*, built by *Sansovino* and *Scarpagnino* between the Grand Canal and the *Church of San Giacomo*, were where business was discussed and deals made. *Thomas Coryat* offers a careful description of what went on there: "*The Rialto which is at the farther side of the bridge as you come from St. Marks, is a most stately building. The building being the Exchange of Venice, where the Venetians, the Gentlemen and the Merchants doe meete twice a day, betwixt eleven and twelve of the clocke in the morning, and betwixt five and sixe of the clocke in the afternoone. This Rialto is of a goodly height, built all with bricke as the Palaces are, adorned with many faire walkes or open galleries, and hath a prety quadrangular court adjoyning to it.*"

The question "*What news on the Rialto?*", which is actually asked twice in *The Merchant of Venice* (and which, significantly, has been adopted as the name of a modern-day international network of Venetian scholars), reminds us how extremely important the city was as a centre of information during the Renaissance.

The area of *Rialto* was also famous for its shops, which were specially decked out when important visitors were in town (for the Ottoman envoys, for example) and where goods of all sorts were produced, like the celebrated helmet chased for Sultan *Suleiman the Magnificent*. Famous too were the cloths and fabrics. In the earliest description of the city in Italian, *Iacopo d'Albizzotto Guidi* wrote admiringly: "*I had better be careful/because at the Rialto, in the Drapperia/they are very good at selling any cloth, / though it doesn't really pay / to listen to the cries of the vendors / when they display their wares on the street*" (*De la condizione di Venezia*, 1442). It was probably here that Petruchio, the domesticator of Kate in *The Taming of the Shrew*, came "to buy apparel 'gainst the wedding-day". In Shakespeare's day the new Rialto Bridge had not long been built to the bold plans of *Andrea Da Ponte*, who designed it as a single span of such height that a galley would be able to pass underneath with its masts lowered. The high cost of the project was offset by the imposition of a toll. Before the new stone bridge at least three wooden bridges had crossed the Grand Canal at this point. The earliest was destroyed in 1310, during a revolt led by the nobleman *Bajamonte Tiepolo*, which also prompted the establishment of the Council of Ten. The second collapsed beneath the weight of the onlookers who had gathered there to see the wedding procession of the Marquis and Marchioness of Ferrara, in 1444. The third, a drawbridge, can be seen in painting by *Carpaccio* in the *Accademia Galleries* (there is a black gondolier in the same picture). In 1524 a competition was announced for a new bridge to be made of stone and entries were submitted by *Michelangelo*, *Sansovino* and *Palladio*. The finances of the Serenissima were at such a low ebb, however, that the city was denied its new bridge for several decades and all three had died by the time *Andrea Da Ponte* was finally commissioned to get on with it almost sixty years later.

Despite the architect's excellent drawings, however, the building of the great arch of the new Rialto Bridge did not go according to plan and the story goes that what the workers managed to put in place during the day regularly collapsed into the Canal after nightfall. The site foreman was a promising youngster called Sebastiano and this was his first important job: he was determined to make a success of the work because it held the key to his future and that of the son his wife Chiara would shortly produce.

Since the incidents always happened at night, Sebastiano decided to stay behind and see what happened. On the stroke of midnight, there was a tremendous crash and a section of the arch toppled into the Grand Canal. The young man felt his blood run cold as there came a mocking laugh just behind him. It was the Devil. «All your work will be to no avail,» he said. «No-one will manage to build this bridge in stone. However, if you wish, I can help you. Of course, there will be a price to pay.» «What do you want of me? My soul?» asked Sebastiano. «Not yours,» said the Devil with a cruel laugh. «I want the soul of the first to cross the bridge once the work has finished.» The young man accepted the terms and the next day he set to work again with his masons and stonecutters. The Devil kept his word: there were no more collapses and eventually the bridge was finished. In the meantime, Sebastiano had an idea. The Devil hadn't stipulated that the first over the bridge had to be a man. So he arranged for a cockerel to be released at daybreak. He placed guards at the sides of the bridge and gave orders that they should let no-one pass. But the Devil had other ideas. Dressed as a workman he knocked at the door of the foreman's house and told Chiara that her husband needed her immediately. She hurried to the site, where the guards recognized her and let her pass. When Sebastiano saw his wife on the bridge, he shuddered with horror and thought that all was lost.

The next day, shortly after the official inauguration ceremony, a servant girl brought him the news that his child was stillborn and that Chiara was close to death. He ran home but too late. Chiara was already dead. From that day, the soul of the baby began to haunt the bridge. As he crossed it one night, an old gondolier heard a tiny sneeze at the top. Though he could see no-one, he called out, as one does, «Bless you!». «Thank you!» came back a child's voice: it was the soul of the baby, saved by the words of the gondolier.

It is said that the Venetian merchants who lived in London at the time of Shakespeare, near the Tower and in Bishopsgate, referred nostalgically to their districts with the names of familiar places and made appointments to meet each other at "San Marco" and "Rialto".

LANCELOT – *The fiend is at mine elbow*
and tempts me, saying to me, "Gobbo, Lancelot Gobbo,
good Lancelot", or "good Gobbo," or "good Lancelot
Gobbo – use your legs, take the start, run away."
[THE MERCHANT OF VENICE, Act II, Scene II]

 ❦ [21] THE "GOBBO DI RIALTO"

he historian *Brian Pullan*, as we shall hear again later, discovered that towards the end of the XVI century, just at the
time scholars lose track of Shakespeare in England (the famous
"lost years"), two of the Christian guards at the entrance to the *Ghetto*
were called *Gobbo*, just like Shylock's servant (Gobbo means "hunchback"
in Italian and it remains a common surname). But the most famous Venetian *Gobbo* is to be found at the Rialto. Next to the *sotoportego del Banco Giro*,
right opposite the *Church of San Giacometto* and beside the entrance to the
law court, there is a stump of an ancient column, from the top of which the
laws were proclaimed in the days of the *Serenissima*. To mount onto this plat-
form the crier had to climb a few stone steps supported by a statue of a
kneeling figure, bent beneath the weight; this, for Venetians is the *Gobbo
di Rialto*, sculpted by *Pietro da Salò* in 1541. Legend has it that the sculpture depicts a hunchback who really existed, who was sentenced to hold up
a similar staircase … and who died from the effort. In actual fact, the statue of the Gobbo is not hunchbacked at all but simply bent under his burden.
From his very earliest days on the spot, the Gobbo unintentionally became the
centre of a curious custom. A kiss on the cheek of the statue came to mark the
end of the torment meted out to thieves and other miscreants who had been
sentenced to be whipped and beaten from St. Mark's to the Rialto.
Then some legal official of the Republic must have decided that the custom
was akin to blasphemy: if anyone was to be thanked and kissed under these

circumstances, it was the patron saint of the city, not a humble hunchback. So on 13th March 1545 a cross surmounted by a lion of St. Mark was carved into the column at the corner with *ruga dei Oresi*. The image is still there and ever since has been known as "the cross of the thrashed".

As for the *Gobbo*, he later became what *Pasquino* and *Marforio* were in Rome: characters over whose name appeared satirical writings that ridiculed people, customs, the State and the clergy. The *Gobbo* would converse with *Marocco Popone*, who was none other than one of the figures at the base of the column supporting the lion in *Piazzetta San Marco*, the one with a water-melon in a wicker basket. Another statue that performed the task of providing a sounding board for public opinion in Venice is mentioned in the chapter dedicated to campo dei Mori: this is sior *Antonio Rioba*, the most famous of the Mastelli brothers.

From 1577 on, various publications purporting to be by the "Gobbo" started to voice opinions on a number of topics of current interest, such as the appearance of comets or the dishonesty of women, and in 1606-07, during the period of the Interdict that brought Venice and Rome into conflict, the *Gobbo* became the "author" of satirical attacks on the Pope.

IAGO – *Even now, now, very now, an old black ram*
Is tupping your white ewe!
[OTHELLO, Act I, Scene I]

LORENZO – *I shall answer that better to the commonwealth*
than you can the getting up of the Negro's belly.
The Moor is with child by you, Lancelot.
[THE MERCHANT OF VENICE, Act III, Scene V]

 [22] **THE ARDENT PASSIONS OF EROS**
hakespeare loved all forms of language, from the most high-
flown to the crudest vernacular, and he delighted in
insinuation, plays on words and puns and ambiguities of a
sexual nature. The best-known examples are his uses of apparently innocent
words such as "*thing*" and "*Will*" (which was also Shakespeare's nickname),
that conceals references to male and female sexual organs. It is a curious fact
that *The Merchant of Venice*, according to *Eric Partridge*, the author of *Shakespeare's Bawdy*, is one of the "cleanest" works in the canon, while *Othello*
features one of the highest incidences of obscenity. It would probably have
amused Shakespeare to see an example of how Venetians too enjoyed a dirty
joke and were not above carving it into the marble facing of the *Palazzo dei
Camerlenghi*, at the foot of the Rialto Bridge.
This handsome building stands on the market side of the Grand Canal.
Erected in 1525 by *Guglielmo Bergamasco*, it housed the offices of the three
Lords of the Venetian Exchequer (the *Camerlenghi* or Chamberlains of its
name) and during the XVI century the ground floor served as the State prison
for debtors and petty criminals. The building is well-known to Venetians
especially for the two capitals nearest the corner on the side facing the bridge.
They contain carvings of two human figures: the man has a strange excres-

cence between his legs and the woman a fire blazing in the same place. According to tradition, these figures were carved when the populous market district was still waiting for the new stone Rialto Bridge that had been promised decades before. People were so disillusioned that one day a man came out with the mocking comment "*The day that bridge is finished I'll find a nail growing between my legs!*", and a woman echoed "*and my pussy will catch fire!*". So when the authorities finally commissioned the work on the oldest bridge still spanning the Grand Canal they had the inevitable fate of the two sceptics depicted on the capitals (also to remind people that the State has eyes and ears everywhere).

At the foot of the bridge on the other side of the Grand Canal there is still a canalside path called *fondamenta del Traghetto del Buso* (from where the ferry "of the hole" used to ply). Most people explain this strange name by reference to the fact that the ferry station occupies such a confined space. But there is another theory, which places an obscene meaning on the word *buso* and relates that it was this ferry that the prostitutes of the city took to return en masse when, in the early 1400s, the authorities were forced by public protest to rescind an order they had given, banning the oldest profession. Since then, to commemorate the triumphal crossing amid the joyful shouts of the boatmen, the ferry route and later the place have been commonly (and coarsely) known by the name of the "merchandise" the women were bringing. Another side to the story comes out in a map of the city dated 1697, where the ferry is named as *dei Ruffiani* and alludes to the boatmen's reputation as the pimps who brought the prostitutes back.

And one last curious example of sexual exploits in Venice concerns an "outsider". This was *Vincenzo Gonzaga* (the future, *Vincenzo I*, *The magnificent*), who, at a certain point in his youth, was obliged to furnish proof of his virility. Vincezo's first marriage, to *Margherita Farnese*, had failed because Margherita was physically unable to bear children.

The union was annulled and the Gonzagas now had plans for him to *Leonora de' Medici*. But the Florentines were suspicious: what if the failure of the previous marriage had been Vincenzo's fault and not Margherita's? After endless wrangling, rather than lose the golden opportunity of such an advantageous match, the Gonzagas arranged for Vincenzo to be put to the test in Venice, where a young Florentine woman was chosen from several aspirants to provide … the test bed. Vincenzo passed with flying colours: the wedding took place and the young Florentine woman, now pregnant, was "compensated" with a dowry of three thousand *scudi* and a husband.

SESTIER
DE S. POLO

PONTE
DE LE TETTE

SOTOPORTEGO
E CORTE DE
CA' BOLLANI

1916

IAGO – *Now will I question Cassio of Bianca,*
A hussy that by selling her desires
Buys herself bread and cloth. It is a creature
That dotes on Cassio – as 'tis the strumpet's plague
To beguile many and be beguiled by one.
[OTHELLO, Act IV, Scene I]

OTHELLO – *I took you for that cunning whore of Venice*
That married with Othello.
[OTHELLO, Act IV, Scene II]

 [23] "MODERN CALYPSOS": COURTESANS AND PROSTITUTES
he courtesans of Venice were famous throughout Europe and
the English traveller *Thomas Coryat* was surprised that the various official descriptions of the city quite ignored the matter.
He even went so far as to state that at the time of his visit there were as many
as twenty thousand of what he euphemistically referred to as "modern
Calypsos", celebrated to the point that their reputation "*hath drawn many
to Venice from some of the remotest parts of Christendome to contemplate their
beauties and enjoy their pleasing dalliances.*"
Coryat's attitude evinces a not uncommon ambivalence: he castigates the
Venetians, who "*should be daily afraid lest their winking at such uncleanness
should be an occasion to draw down upon them God's curses and vengeance from
Heaven, and to consume their city with fire and brimstone, as in time past he did
Sodome and Gomorrha*". But at the same time he wastes no time in visiting
one of these courtesans, both because he wishes to convert her and because
he thinks "*that a virtuous man will be the more confirmed and settled in virtue
by the observation of some vices then if he did not at all know what they were*".
Shakespeare doesn't fail to bring this well-known side of Venice to the stage,

but the description of Bianca suggests a common sex worker rather than one of the legendary courtesans, who were famous for their cultural sophistication, artistic talent and high-class clientele. Indeed, prostitution in Venice operated according to a very complex hierarchy.

During the 1500s in fact, a quite separate category of prostitute became established in the city; as well as physical attractions, refined amatory skills and supreme elegance they could offer their highly placed clients an extensive knowledge of art, music and literature, gleaned also from their acquaintance with painters, architects, men of power and influence, writers. A sort of elite: a group of women leading independent, intellectually stimulating (though not always happy or easy) lives of considerable luxury; many were famous and what we might now call fashion icons. According to the chronicler Marin Sanudo, at the beginning of the XVI century there were 11,654 official courtesans in Venice.

A few decades later, the practice of sex for payment had become such a firmly rooted feature of the social fabric of the city that a guide to Venetian prostitutes was published. This was the "*Catalogue of all the principal and most famous courtesans in Venice; their names and the names of their bawds, the apartments and districts where they live and the amount of money a gentleman has to pay to enjoy their favours ...*". Some of the courtesans in the catalogue were married and 37 of them used the services of their mother to procure them clients; others had no procuress and are described in the book as: "*Madam Just-knock-on-my-door*". Some charged as much as 25 or 30 scudi, such as "*Livia Azzalina at San Marziale; procuress, Maria Visentina et Meneghina; address, corte de Ca' Badoer al ponte dei Sassini, rate 25 scudi. Paolina Fila Canevo at Santa Lucia; procuress, one of her servants; rate 30 scudi*". The married courtesans included "*Andriana Schiavonetta at Santa Fosca, a married woman; procuress, her mother; rate 4 scudi. Caterina da Todi, a married woman at San Vio; procuress, her servant; rate 1 scudo*".

The least popular courtesans charged just half a *scudo*. The booklet concludes with the statistic: "*...there are 215 of these ladies altogether and anyone*

who wishes to be entertained by all of them will have to pay 1,200 gold scudi …".
At least one of these women, an archetypal courtesan whose fame has lasted down the centuries, really deserves a chapter to herself. *Veronica Franco* was born in Venice in about 1546. She married young, to a doctor, but soon began her career as a courtesan. Uninhibited, charming and adventurous as well as a writer, musician and poetess, she kept open house for painters, musicians and literary figures and granted them her favours in exchange for writings and philosophical discussions. Veronica was well known far beyond the confines of the Venetian state: the King of France, *Henri III*, paid her a call as he was passing through Venice in 1574 and so entranced was he by her beauty that he took a portrait of her away with him.

In short, Veronica skilfully combined the sale of her body with cultural refinement. Some of her poetic and literary compositions (including the *Terze rime* and *Friendly letters*) were much admired by her contemporaries and are still worth their place in any anthology of the literature of the time.

Another turning point came when she reached forty: in 1580, with the help of a number of noblemen, she founded a refuge for repentant courtesans, the "*Casa del Soccorso*" near the *Church of the Carmini*. Sympathetic assistance was provided by other former courtesans, who understood the feelings and problems they were experiencing; many married, took vows or employment in a household.

But the history of prostitution in Venice goes back much further. In 1360, a state-run brothel called the *Castelletto* was established in a group of houses in the area of *Sant'Aponal*. This "little fortress" was so called because it was

---

Business was not always so brisk for Venetian courtesans. On the contrary. In the mid-XV century, a number of them started a fashion of wearing their hair brushed to the centre of the forehead to form a sort of quiff. The result was that they looked more like young men, and the Council of Ten, ever wary of encouraging "unnatural vice", decreed the fashion illegal on 14th March 1470. And some years later, on 27th March 1511, they appealed directly to no less a figure than the Patriarch, *Antonio Contarini*; they could no longer make a living, they said, because "*niun va li lboro*" – no-one would go with them any more.

watched over by six guards and run with military efficiency. A sort of red-light district where the authorities, in order to distract men from the vice of sodomy, required prostitutes to stand at the doors or windows, lasciviously *décolletées* and illuminated by oil-lamps after dark. In practice a precursor of the modern peep-show, and indeed, not far away, there is still a bridge and a canal-side path whose name, *de le Tette*, recalls this "up-front" practice. So it should come as no surprise if the "foreigner" Othello, his imagination infected by Iago, who says of Venetian women that "*they do let God see the pranks / They dare not show their husbands; their best conscience / Is not to leave't undone, but keep't unknown*", is tormented by the suspicion that his innocent wife is really a woman of easy virtue, "*Was this fair paper, this most goodly book / Made to write 'whore' upon?*". But the last word must go these celebrated women themselves, so often believed to be the sole mistresses of their own destiny. In her *Friendly letters*, published in 1580, *Veronica Franco* wrote as follows to a mother who had ambitions for her daughter to become a courtesan: "*There is no more unhappy, or indeed senseless, thing than to subject one's body and one's efforts to servitude of a kind that frightens me just to think of it. To offer oneself as a prey to all and sundry, to risk being cheated, robbed, even killed and from one day to the next lose everything one has worked long and hard to get, with so many other dangers of injury and horrifying disease; to eat with someone else's mouth, to sleep with someone else's eyes, to move as someone else commands, knowing that the inevitable outcome will be the ruin of one's faculties and one's life*".

OTHELLO – *And say besides that in Aleppo once,*
Where a malignant and a turbaned Turk
Beat a Venetian and traduced the state,
I took by th'throat the circumcised dog
And smote him – thus!
[OTHELLO, Act V, Scene II]

DUKE – ... *and pluck commiseration of his state*
From brassy bosoms and rough hearts of flint,
From stubborn Turks and Tartars, never train'd
To offices of tender courtesy.
[THE MERCHANT OF VENICE, Act IV, Scene I]

 ☞ [24] THE TURKS IN VENICE

ll the events dramatised in *Othello* take place in the looming shadow of a conflict with the Turks (subsequently avoided thanks to a providential storm) which obliges the newly-wed Desdemona and Othello to rush straight to Cyprus. The Turks were Venice's great adversaries in the Mediterranean, infidel enemies, a great rival empire, but also trading partners who were not above commissioning the gold- and silversmiths of the Rialto to make a legendary helmet as a gift for one Sultan, or *Gentile Bellini* to paint the portrait of his son and successor; and there was a substantial Venetian community resident in Constantinople.

Paolo Paruta, the official historian of the Serenissima, was typical in his depiction of the Turks: he gave an example of how they need to be understood as barbarians but he also added a pragmatic explanation of how best to conduct commercial relations with them. When the Englishman *William Thomas* stated in his *Historie of Italie* (1549) that foreigners enjoyed such freedom in Venice that "*If thou be a Jewe, a Turke, or beleeuest in the diuell (so thou spreade not thyne opinions abroade) thou arte free from all con-trollement...*" he used the word "*Turke*" to mean any Moslem, while in Venice "*Turk*" meant any subject of the Ottoman Empire and could thus refer to several very different peoples, not all of them Moslem.

Even in the aftermath of the *Battle of Lepanto* of 1571, an overwhelming victory for the European powers (though it didn't stop the Ottoman Empire retaking Othello's Cyprus just two years later), "Turks" continued to live in Venice. Following the news of the defeat suffered by their fleet, seventy-five of them gathered in the house of the diplomatic representative *Marcantonio Barbaro*, fearing they might be attacked by Venetians roused by the victory. After this experience many of them, especially those who came from the Balkans and Greece, sought a place in Venice where they could live together, after the exam-ple of the Ghetto. Despite the peace treaty between the "Sublime Porte" and the Serenissima signed in 1573, we know that the two envoys *Hasan* and *Haci Mustafa* took refuge in an inn near the *Ponte della Paglia*, beside the Doge's Palace, because a mob (and even some soldiers) were hurling insults and trying to assault them until Haci brandished a scimitar and put their assailants to flight. A first *fondaco* or trading post was established in 1575 on the premises of the *Osteria all'Angelo* (the Angel Inn) at *San Matteo di Rialto*; the chosen site was conveniently near the market but safely situated in a narrow *calle* (the modern visitor who does track down *Calle dell'Angelo* will suddenly step back in time almost to another age). As noted by Maria Pia Pedani, an expert on the "Turkish" and Moslem presence in Venice, there were many inns and taverns in the Rialto district that were patronized by lower class "foreigners": the area had a grim reputation and was known as "*inhon-estissimo*". Thus the Moslems (like the Jews) were relegated to the margins of society and at the same time kept near the centre of commerce.

But although Venetians made no attempt to disguise their opinions, and placed all Ottomans on the same level (and it was mainly Albanians and other inhabitants of the Balkans who lived in the parish of San Matteo), some Anatolian merchants took exception to their "Turkish" co-tenants (from Greece and Bosnia) and changed their lodgings. In 1621, having taken almost half a century to examine various alternative proposals, the Senate finally designated the ancient *palazzo Palmieri da Pesaro*, on the Grand Canal, as the new *Fondaco dei Turchi*.

To give an idea of the complexity of the relations between the "Winged Lion" and the "Crescent Moon" throughout the 1500s, we need go no further than the story of *Cecilia Venier Baffo*, a second cousin of Doge *Sebastiano Venier*, who became… a Sultana. Cecilia was born on Paros around 1525, the daughter of the Venetian governor of the island, *Nicolò Venier*. She had scarcely turned twelve years of age when she was kidnapped by *Hayreddin Barbarossa* while sailing from Venice to Corfù to join her father; she was assigned to the harem of *Suleiman the Magnificent* and later became the favourite wife of his son *Selim II*, with the name *Nur Banì*, which means "Lady of Splendour", "Lady of Light"; celebrated for her beauty, Cecilia was also known as *Selifè*, the "Pure One". When Selim died she became the Sultana Mother, the *Validè*, and as such exercised huge influence over her son *Murad III*. This also worked to the advantage of the Venetians, for example when she persuaded Murad to defer his plans to take the Island of Candia (present-day Crete) on the grounds that she did not want to be at war with her homeland. She maintained constant relations with the *Serenissima* and the Venetian archives still conserve her correspondence, such as the note sent to Doge *Nicolò Da Ponte* in 1582, where she says that

Curiously the institution of *fondaco* (the word in itself is multicultural, deriving from the Arabic word *funduq*, which in turn came from the Greek *pandocheion*, inn), which in Venice was not only a trading post but also a place of residence for merchants and a warehouse for their goods, echoed the Islamic model of a district destined for a specific ethnic group, where they would be safe and could pursue their own way of life. Indeed, within the *Fondaco dei Turchi* there was a *Hammam* (a Turkish bath) and the Venetians were astonished at how clean and salubrious the building was. But the purity of the place did not prevent suspicions of relations between Moslems and Christian prostitutes (prohibited by law) and rumours of children being kidnapped.

her memories of Venice are such that she is prepared to grant it any favour. Other letters contain frivolous, even rather peculiar requests, which the Republic nevertheless hastened to satisfy. For example, the Validè wrote to *Francesco Morosini*, then *Bailo* of Constantinople, that she had received two dogs from Venice: "*but*," she complained, "*I don't need big hunting hounds, what I want are small white lapdogs…*". But she also asked for a number of "*cushions in beautiful, elaborate cloth of gold,* […] *and lined with silk or damask or satin brocatelle*", and for others in double width woollen cloth. The *Bailo* passed the message on to the Senate, which duly set aside two thousand *zecchini* for the purchase of gifts for the Sultana Mother. This in fact is the last time the State records speak of *Cecilia Venier*, for the Venetian Sultana died on 7th December of that year.

Of course Venice also preserves many memories of the battles it fought against the "Sublime Porte". The *Church of SS. Giovanni e Paolo* still conserves (in an urn inside a monument) the skin of *Marcantonio Bragadin*, the determined and courageous defender of Famagusta, who was flayed alive by the Turks in 1571, a few weeks before the *Battle of Lepanto*. Stolen from the Arsenal at Constantinople, where it was displayed as a trophy, the skin was initially kept in the *Church of San Gregorio* before being moved to its present resting place in 1596. "*It was folded to the size of a sheet of paper,*" – says a contemporary chronicle – "*firm and soft as if it were a piece of cloth; one could still see the hairs on his chest, and some flesh was still attached to the fingers of the right hand and the finger nails looked as if they might still be growing*".

When Othello commits suicide, comparing himself to a "*malignant… Turk, …a circumcised dog*", he uses a crusading tone that seems to characterize his zeal as a converted Christian, the same attitude as that of the copious amounts of Venetian propaganda in which the Turk figured as the Antichrist and the cruel impaler; the Turk had banished Venus from Cyprus and, to the horror of the Venetian aristocracy, conferred high office and dignity on low-born men. But as the historian *Gino Benzoni* has written, Turks and Venetians always remained "brothers-enemies" and there was a bizarrely irrepressible movement of men and things between the two empires even when relations were at their worst.

OTELLO – *By the world,*
I think my wife be honest, and think she is not.
I think that thou art just, and think thou art not.
[OTHELLO, Act III, Scene III]

LANCELOT – *My conscience hanging about the neck of my heart*
says very wisely to me, 'My honest friend Launcelot',
being an honest man's son or rather an honest woman's son…
[THE MERCHANT OF VENICE, Act II, Scene II]

EMILIA – *'Tis not a year or two shows us a man.*
They are all but stomachs, and we all but food:
To eat us hungerly, and when they are full
They belch us.
[OTHELLO, Act III, Scene IV]

 [25] THE HONEST WOMAN

he word "*honest*" recurs as many as fifty-two times in *Othello*, to the point, according to the eminent critic *William Empson*, where it ceases to be a simple adjective and becomes a study in the semantic ambiguity of a single word. Until the end of the tragedy, Othello insists on calling the man who is deceiving him "honest Iago", and Iago sets his infernal strategy in motion by instilling doubt about Desdemona's faithfulness in Othello's mind through his echoing of the word: when Othello asks him about Cassio, "*Is he not honest?*", Iago replies, "*Honest, my lord?*".

It is tempting to imagine that Shakespeare might have thought of the ambiguity of the concept while looking at the stone face of a woman, set into the wall of a house, who provides the name for a canalside path and a bridge near the Basilica of the Frari – "*the Honest Woman*".

There are in fact two legends that claim to explain the origins of this unusual place name. The first has more to do with local gossip and recounts that this was the home of a prostitute, whose rooms could be reached by a discreetly hidden staircase and whose rates were highly competitive – honest, in other words. And when a Venetian wants to make a dig at the fair sex, one says that the only honest woman in Venice is the one in stone overlooking the *Ponte della Donna Onesta*.

But there is also the appealing legend that tells of the virtues of Santina, an exquisitely beautiful woman from Murano, the wife of the master sword maker Battista. A young nobleman called Marchetto Rizzo had fallen in love with Santina and in order to gain entrance to the sword maker's house and seduce his wife had commissioned the man to make him a small dagger, called a *misericordia*. Taking good care to call only when he was sure the husband was away, the young man dropped by regularly to ask whether the weapon was ready and tried all his wiles to undermine the defences of the woman. But Santina never gave in to Rizzo's blandishments. The time came when the dagger was in fact ready and since he no longer had an excuse to continue pestering the woman, Rizzo simply took her by force. Having lost her honour and not wanting to live with the shame of it, the beautiful Santina grasped the dagger that her husband had made for the young man and plunged it into her heart in despair.

The whole story would leave an unpleasant taste in the mouth if it were not that the court reports of the day fortunately give us a glimpse of quite a different outcome: a friend of the sword maker, a shopkeeper called Zuane, had for some time been suspicious of the assiduous nature of Marchetto Rizzo's visits and had decided to keep a close check on his movemements: he surprised the young man just as he was overpowering his victim, and struck him with the just finished dagger. Though he saved Santina and did not kill Rizzo, the latter was banished for six months on 14th October 1490. Support for this latter version of events comes not only from the date of Zuane's conviction but also from the name of a street just a couple of hundred metres away – *calle de l'Amor degli Amici* (the street of loving friendship) – where Zuane had his shop.

Though Shakespeare makes Iago a notorious misogynist, his wife Emilia is given a speech of such violent invective that she has been described as an early feminist. In this connection it is also worth remembering that there were many cultivated female figures who during and immediately after Shakespeare's time produced a lively literary output that did not shrink from denouncing the impositions and wrongs of the "unfair" sex.

Between the XVI and XVII centuries, numerous female literary talents came to the fore in Venice: not only *Veronica Franco*, already mentioned in the chapter dedicated to courtesans, but also *Arcangela Tarabotti*, *Gaspara Stampa* and *Moderata Fonte*, three women who differed markedly from each other. The first, who had been compelled to enter a nunnery, expressed her rejection of the rules of the convent life that her father had forced on her through two books: *Paternal tyranny* and *The inferno of nunhood*. Eventually she became resigned to her circumstances and in later life wrote a number of works inspired by asceticism.

Gaspara Stampa died at the age of thirty-one, after meeting and falling in love with *Collaltino di Collalto*: at first her love was returned but then he abandoned her and she poured all her desperate passion into what became one of the most famous collections of poems of the 1500s, *Rime d'amore*. She also asserted her freedom and vitality through many other love affairs.

Moderata Fonte (whose real name was *Modesta Pozzo*), was orphaned as a child. She was brought up by her grandparents and learned to read and write in Latin, to draw, sing and play both the lute and the harpsichord. During her ten years of marriage to *Filippo Zorzi*, she had little time to develop her literary skills, but before she died, giving birth to her fourth child, at the age of thirty-seven, she managed to finish her greatest work, *The merit of women*, which was published posthumously in 1600. And we must not forget the first woman ever to graduate, the Venetian *Elena Lucrezia Corner Piscopia*, whose scholarly feats are mentioned in the chapter dedicated to the entourage of intellectuals who gravitated around the *Ridotto Morosini*.

SHYLOCK – *What judgement shall I dread, doing no wrong?*
You have among you many a purchased slave
Which, like your asses and your dogs and mules,
You use in abject and in slavish parts,
Because you bought them. Shall I say to you
"Let them be free, marry them to your heirs.
Why sweat they under burdens? Let their beds
Be made as soft as yours, and let their palates
Be seasoned with such viands." You will answer "The slaves are ours."
[THE MERCHANT OF VENICE, Act IV, Scene I]

OTHELLO – *Wherein I spoke of most disastrous chances,*
Of moving accidents by flood and field,
Of hair-breadth scapes i'th' imminent deadly breach,
Of being taken by the insolent foe
And sold to slavery, of my redemption thence...
[OTHELLO, Act I, Scene III]

 ☞ [26] CIAO, SLAVES AND SLAVS

hen two people exchange a *ciao* in the streets of Venice – as everywhere else in Italy and, indeed, in many other parts of the world – they probably don't know that the etymology of this most informal of greetings takes us back, through the respectful Venetian salutation *s-ciao* meaning "I am your servant", to the word "*schiavo*", a slave. Though nowhere in the city retains any association with slavery, the practice was deeply rooted in the city, where there was a market for slaves from the Balkans (which gave rise to another etymological issue – the possible connection between the words *Slavi* and *schiavi*, Slavs and slaves) and from Africa. And although the slave auctions at the Rialto were banned in 1366, Venice continued to import them and tolerate their sale by private treaty, if not by auction. A law of 1381 decreed that a cargo ship could carry up to four slaves for every crew member, so a vessel with 50 sailors could transport 200 slaves. In 1416, there is a record of the purchase of a black slave with a curiously Shakespearian name: "*Negro I, name Anziloto* (Lancelot), *received for the ship of Signor Stefano di Marin,* [...] *for Signor Piero Bembo for the stipulated price of 36, k. 16, val k. 22 per ducat, £3 6s. 11d.*".

In 1489 the Senate instituted punitive measures to deal with the phenomenon of runaway black slaves: rewards were promised to anyone who captured a fugitive, and immunity from prosecution if the slave should be killed during the chase. At the very time the practice of slavery was declining in Venice, during Shakespeare's lifetimes, it was starting to increase in England so perhaps Shylock's invective would have carried more weight with the London audience than with his Venetian judges.

The slave trade at this time was not all in one direction. As the historian *Robert C. Davis* eloquently puts it: "*by the end of the sixteenth century slave-hunting corsair galleys roamed throughout the Mediterranean, seeking their human booty from Catalonia to Egypt. Men and women, Turks and Moors, Jews and Catholics, Protestant and Orthodox–all were potential victims, to be seized and eventually herded into the slave pens of Constantinople, Algiers, Tunis, Tripoli, Malta, Naples, or Livorno and to be resold as galley oarsmen, agricultural labourers, or house slaves*".

In 1586, in common with other Italian cities, Venice set up a State Office – the *Provveditori sopra Ospedali e Luoghi Pii* – to collect the funds needed to ransom the large number of Venetian prisoners of war whom the Ottomans had sold into slavery. But despite a number of impassioned sermons by the Patriarch, appealing for charitable donations to the cause, public response was tepid and by 1612, there remained only four of the sixteen collection boxes placed in Venetian churches in 1586 and altogether they yielded the miserable sum of eleven ducats a year (plus the odd foreign coin and others that were too worn to be acknowledged as legal currency by the Mint).

There are numerous accounts of both African and Turkish slaves, who were used not only on Venetian galleys but also as household servants to noble families. The art historian *Paul Kaplan* has studied the many examples of African slaves and servants featuring in Venetian and Italian Renaissance art. The most striking instance of the phenomenon occurs later than Shakespeare, however, and comes in the monument to Doge *Giovanni Pesaro* (1669) in the *Basilica di Santa Maria Gloriosa dei Frari*. Sculpted by *Melchiorre Barthel* and *Bernardo Falcone* to designs by *Baldassarre Longhena*, this majestic work features the Doge seated beneath an elaborate canopy, flanked by allegorical figures representing virtues; the heavy frame surrounding the celebratory group rests on cushions, which in turn are supported by four statues of black men in ragged clothes, bowed and visibly grimacing at the effort. More effectively than any other, the work depicts a society in which power and morals depend literally on the oppressive work of black slaves. According to local tradition, the sculptor committed suicide when he realized, when the work was completed, that he had made the cushions too plump for them to convey a realistic impression of the weight they were supporting; evidently far more a matter of shame than the presence of the four slaves shouldering the cushions.

Amongst the most famous slaves of the time was *Miguel de Cervantes*, who was held prisoner in Algiers for several years. As regards possible references to Shakespeare, however, the most important was *Hasan ben Mohammed al-Wazzan al-Zaiyati*, who was born in Granada around 1485 and moved to Fez in 1492 with the fall of the last Islamic state in mainland Spain. This learned scholar and diplomat made several long journeys across North Africa and, in 1517, was captured by corsairs off the coast of Djerba as he was returning from a mission to Egypt. At first he was taken to Naples as a slave, but on recognition of his extraordinary intelligence he was sent to Rome as a gift to *Pope Leo X*.

In 1520, he was converted and baptized with the Pope's name, Johannes Leo, which in turn gave rise to the nickname by which he was known all over Europe: *Leo Africanus*. At the moment of his capture he had with him the draft of the work that was to make him famous, *The History and Description of Africa*. This was translated into English in 1600 and remained the main source of Europeans' knowledge of Africa until the great explorations of the 1800's, and almost certainly of many of the details mentioned in *Othello*.

OTHELLO – *Come, Desdemona. I have but an hour*
Of love, of worldly matter and direction
To spend with thee. We must obey the time.
[OTHELLO, Act I, Scene III]

 ✒ [27] **OTHELLO'S HOUSE**

A t no point in the tragedy does Shakespeare mention Othello's home, (indeed, he describes his soldiering circumstances as "unhoused free condition") and we are not told whether the few hours he manages to spend with Desdemona after their secret wedding are spent at the *Sagittario* (see the chapter dedicated to the *Frezzeria*) or in some Venetian *palazzo* (as envisaged by *Caryl Phillips* in his novel *The Nature of Blood*). Yet some of the most popular guides to Venice unhesitatingly point to a building in *campo dei Carmini*, not far from the busy *campo Santa Margherita* in the district of *Dorsoduro*, as "the house of the Moor"; there is a statue of a soldier on the landward façade and a blackened helmeted head overlooking the canal. The attribution probably dates from the XIX century, one of *Rawdon Brown's* flights of fancy (for more on Brown, see the note to the chapter devoted to *Thomas de Mowbray*, the first Duke of Norfolk).

The nobleman *Cristoforo Moro* was posted as lieutenant of Cyprus in 1505 and returned to Venice three years later as the commander of fourteen galleys from Candia (Creta). His wife died during the voyage home and in 1515 he married a daughter of *Donato da Lezze* whose nickname was "*Demonio Bianco*" (white demon), which might later have been transformed into Desdemona. Then the surname *Moro* might be a corruption of *Guoro*, a family that a family that acquired the *palazzo* from the Civrans around this time. In taking the plot of his celebrated tragedy from *Gli Hecatommithi* by the Italian *Giambattista Giraldi Cinzio*, published in 1565, Shakespeare followed his source in making his leading character a dark-skinned Moor rather than *Moro* by name, the assumption being that Cinzio was concerned not to offend the Venetian nobility. According to another version, the figure of Othello could have been inspired by that of *Nicola Contarini*, the heroic defender of Venetian possessions from the Turks. He was said to have had a dark complexion (given the volume of trade with the East, many Venetians were of mixed race); Contarini's story had quite a different outcome, however, for he was the victim of a murder rather than the perpetrator; and when he was killed, *Palma Querini*, his wife, had already returned to her family in order to escape her husband's extreme jealousy (he had tried to strangle her). The couple were married in 1535 and the difference in their ages was similar to that between Othello and Desdemona. But pace *Rawdon Brown* and authoritative writers such as *Giuseppe Tomasi di Lampedusa* who accepted his version, the character in *Gli Hecatommithi* is a "Moor" by ethnic origin rather than by name and the idea that Cinzio tinkered with the facts in order to avoid offending the Moro family is contradicted by the clear moralistic intention of the novella, which deliberately portrays a racially mixed marriage in order to discourage unions contracted against the wishes of parents and with men "*whom nature, Heaven and way of life have made different from us*" and it is difficult think otherwise when Cinzio's Desdemona, reacting to the furious jealousy of her husband, retorts: "*But you Moors are by nature hot-tempered, so anything little thing can arouse you to anger and vendetta*".

SALERIO – *But there the Duke was given to understand*
That in a gondola were seen together
Lorenzo and his amorous Jessica.
[THE MERCHANT OF VENICE, Act II, Scene VIII]

RODERIGO – *…your fair daughter,*
At this odd-even and dull watch o' th' night,
Transported with no worse nor better guard,
But with a knave of common hire, a gondolier,
To the gross clasps of a lascivious Moor.
[OTHELLO, Act I, Scene I]

ROSALIND – *Farewell, Monsieur Traveller. Look you lisp,*
and wear strange suits; disable all the benefits of your
own country; be out of love with your nativity, and
almost chide God for making you that countenance
you are, or I will scarce think you have swam in a gondola.
[AS YOU LIKE IT, Act IV, Scene I]

 [28] GONDOLAS AND GONDOLIERS

t is only to be expected, when his plays speak of Venice, that Shakespeare should mention the boat that has typified Venetian transport for over a thousand years - the *gondola*. Though the oldest known document to include the word *Gondolam* is a decree issued by Doge *Vitale Falier* in 1094, legend has it that as early as 809 Estrella, the beautiful daughter of another doge, *Angelo Partecipazio*, used one to go and meet King *Pipin*, the son of the great *Charlemagne*, in an effort to persuade him to refrain from pursuing the Venetians, who had retreated to the islands of Rialto after the Franks had conquered Malamocco.

Estrella failed in her attempt for Pipin was indifferent to the grace and charm of "the Rose of Venice" and pressed on in an enterprise that proved his undoing: a high tide submerged the causeway he had built to carry his troops to the assault on the enemy and the Venetians easily weathered the storm. But the legend nevertheless had a tragic end: as Estrella was arriving at Rialto to the cheers of the victors, a stone, shot by mistake from a catapult, pierced a hole in her gondola and she disappeared below the waves. The *Rialto Bridge* now stands at the spot where she was lost.

Thomas Coryat reports that there were thirteen ferry stations where gondolas were used for a passenger transport service, and he seems to confirm the questionable reputation that Shakespeare attributes to the gondoliers who carried Desdemona to Othello's arms: "*the boatmen that attend at this ferry are the most vicious and licentious varlets about all the City. For if a stranger entereth into one of their Gondolas, and doth not presently tell them whither he will goe, they will incontinently carry him of their owne accord to a religious house forsooth, where his plumes shall be well pulled before he commeth forth againe. […] if the passenger commandeth them to carry him to any place where his serious and urgent businesse lies, which he cannot but follow without some prejudice unto him, these impious miscreants will either strive to carry him away, maugre his hart, to some irreligious place whether he would not goe, or at the least tempt him with their diabolicall perswasions.*"

As the detail of *Carpaccio*'s celebrated painting *The Miracle of the True Cross* show, many of the gondoliers were African. And the famous diarist *Marin Sanudo*, writing in 1493, tells us that the gondolas were "*rowed by black Saracens or other servants who know how to row … and those servants who are not slaves are paid a wage*".

The *gondola* is about 11 metres long; it is painted black, with seven coats of paint made up to a secret recipe. The colour was established by decree on 8th October 1562, regularly renewed over the decades until 1633; before then, gondolas were richly decorated and coloured and the Serenissima standardized the colour in order to stop noble families vying with each other to flaunt the finest, most luxurious gondola. At this time there were at least ten thousand gondolas in Venice, all of them with the removable cabin (now no longer used) called a *felze*. The gondola has a flat bottom and a slightly assymetrical shape to offset the weight of the gondolier, who rows with a single oar, standing on one side of the stern. Every gondola comprises about 280 wooden parts. The ornamental metal beak or *ferro* has six teeth, which represent the six districts into which the city is divided; the seventh, on the other side, signifies the *island of Giudecca*. Between the six teeth there are often three openwork elements to recall the *islands of Murano, Burano* and *Torcello*. The rounded part above the six teeth echoes the shape of the Doge's horned cap, the *corno* or *zoia*, a symbol of his power and protection of the city. The rest of the *ferro*, which tapers to finish under the gondola, stands for the Grand Canal. Gondolas can be seen all over Venice, but the only *squero* – a boatyard where gondolas are built and maintained – that still pursues its activity in a traditional Venetian boatyard building is the one at San Trovaso, near the Zattere.

Just behind the squero is the elegant *Campo San Trovaso*. In 1934 the square was the scene of a historic production of *The Merchant of Venice*, directed by the famous *Max Reinhardt* and with a cast list featuring the foremost Italian actors of the day. With the magnificent scenery and the evocative power of the setting (a real boat entered the scene along the canal), the production was a tremendous success.

ANTONIO – *I hold the world but as the world, Graziano—*
A stage where every man must play a part,
And mine a sad one.
[THE MERCHANT OF VENICE, Act I, Scene I]

 [29] THE "THEATRE OF THE WORLD"
If Shakespeare ever came to Venice we can be sure that he will
have gone to the theatre. Unfortunately, the open-air stages
of his day no longer exist: the first enclosed theatre was a
wooden construction designed by the great architect *Andrea Palladio* in the
entrance hall of the *Convento della Carità* in 1565. Until then Venice's rich
and lively theatrical life was played out on collapsible stages in the reception
rooms and courtyards of *palazzi* and convents. A few years later the first permanent theatre for plays, elliptical in shape, was built at *San Cassiano*, near
the Rialto market and not far from *calle del Campanile*. Then another
appeared nearby and the street names around the first began referring to the
old theatre, which was eventually closed down and demolished before 1750.
Theatres didn't have an easy time of it in the 1500s. After a first decree banning them in 1508, the Council of Ten closed all theatres in 1581 following
the pressure exerted by a moralizing campaign mounted by the Jesuits and
with explicit reference to the licentious behaviour seen at places such as San
Cassiano. Following a long series of temporary repeals and new bans, the
end of the Interdict imposed by Pope *Paul V* (also mentioned in the final
chapter) finally saw full-scale theatrical activity finally start up again in 1607,
heralding a glorious chapter in the history of the theatre.
The traveller Thomas Coryat, who was in Venice in 1608, drew a generally
unfavourable comparison between Venetian theatres and those he knew in
England, but in Venice he saw something that would not have been allowed
at home: "*I was at one of their Play-houses where I saw a Comedie acted. The*

house is very beggarly and base in comparison of our stately Play-houses in England: neyther can their Actors compare with us for apparell, shewes and musicke. Here I observed certaine things that I never saw before. Women actors. For I saw women acte, a thing that I never saw before, though I have heard that it hath beene sometimes used in London, and they performed it with as good a grace, action, gesture, and whatsoever convenient for a Player, as ever I saw any masculine Actor."

Another entertainment that Shakespeare might have enjoyed in Venice was the *"Teatro del mondo"*; the image of the world as a theatre is one that he uses in various plays, including *The Merchant of Venice* and *As You Like It* (*"All the world's a stage, And all the men and women merely players"*), and which would have been seen by playgoers at the Globe Theatre in the form of the Latin aphorism *Totus mundus agit histrionem*. The *Teatro del mondo* in Venice was a majestic float drawn by marine creatures, which the famous architect *Vincenzo Scamozzi* designed for the festivities organized to celebrate the coronation of the Dogaressa *Morosina Grimani* (1597) and which can still be seen in a contemporary engraving by *Giacomo Franco*.

The theatre at San Cassiano was the first to present a musical work for the paying public rather than the members of a Court or an aristocratic circle; this was *Andromeda* by *Francesco Manelli* and it took place during the Carnival of 1637. Shakespeare had been dead for over twenty years: before long, the fizzing vitality of the Elizabethan play-house would be suppressed by Parliament; in Venice, by contrast, the pits and boxes were just starting to be patronized by the humbler social classes.

A WORLD ON THE FRINGE

LANCELOT – *Turn up on your right hand at the next turning,*
but at the next turning of all, on your left, marry at
the very next turning, turn of no hand but turn down
indirectly to the Jew's house.
GOBBO – *By God's sonties, 'twill be a hard way to hit.*
[THE MERCHANT OF VENICE, Act II, Scene II]

 ✒ [30] THE GHETTO

hakespeare never mentions the Ghetto, the Jewish quarter, but
if one thing may convince Venetians that Shakespeare had first-
hand knowledge of their city, it is the mischievous directions
Lancelot gives to his blind father Gobbo. Bewildered tourists may meet the
same fate today as they ask local children for a specific destination when their
zealous interpretation of maps and signs fails them in the baffling maze of *calli*
and canals. So there is no harm in imagining a disorientated young Shakespeare
roaming around the most famous city in Christendom, getting lost and find-
ing himself in a large, churchless square towards its northwestern edge.
"*Ghetto*", the word which has become synonymous with ethnic segregation,
originated here. In 1516 the city Council decreed the removal of the Jews, who
had fled to the city after the rout of Venice at the *battle of Agnadello, e corpore*
civitatis ("from the body of the city"). Two different proposals were made: that
all these newcomers should be concentrated either on the *island of the*
Giudecca (whose name has nothing to do with Jews, contrary to a widely held
belief) or in *Murano*, the latter a possibility which invites amusing speculations
on a parallel universe of successful Jewish glass-blowers.
It was finally decided to confine the Jews in the former "Public Copper Foundry"
(*Geto del rame del nostro Comun*) for the manufacture of cannon, securing their
services but keeping them safely at the margins, the traditional receptacle of all evil
and perversity (like theatres and brothels). It is not clear whether it was the early

[151]

German foundry workers or the incoming German Jews who, by gutturalizing the initial "G", turned the Getto into the Ghetto. Another curious feature is that the "New" Ghetto is older than the "Old" part. This arises from the simple fact that the Jews were first settled on the island where the most recent foundries had been built. So for Venetians, it was always the "*Geto Novo*".

Constrained within the narrow limits of an island, surrounded by water, multiethnic and multilingual thanks to the five ethnic groups of Jews who had arrived in different waves from Germany, Italy, Spain, Portugal and the Ottoman Empire, the Ghetto became at once a place of segregation and a safe haven for refugees, possibly the best compromise for that time.

Nearly three centuries after Shakespeare, the American consul *William Dean Howells* visited the Ghetto, by now a dilapidated area in a Venice under Austrian rule, and saw the Jews, emancipated by Napoleon in 1797, as ordinary citizens. "*Shylock is dead,*" he wrote in his lively account, *Venetian Life*. "*If he were alive now, Antonio would certainly not spit upon his gorgeous pantaloons or his Parisian coat, as he met him on the Rialto; rather he would probably call out to him, — Ciò Shylock! Bon dì! Go piaser vederla* [Good morning, Shylock, nice to see you]." Less than a century later, Howells' words, "Shylock is dead", ominously acquired a different ring. In 1938 the Racial Laws of the Fascist regime excluded all Jewish citizens from the social and economic life of the country and paved the way for their deportation in 1943-44. In Venice, two hundred people were taken and only eight came back from the death camps: their names can be read today on the memorial to Holocaust victims in the *Campo del Ghetto Nuovo*.

The new arrivals were given permission to build their places of worship as long as they were not immediately recognizable from outside; which explains why the older Venetian synagogues are incorporated into residential buildings.

When the Jews entered the Ghetto, where rental fees immediately rocketed, they had to make a virtue of necessity. Blocks became taller and the head-room in apartments much lower: six or seven-storey buildings had to accommodate as many as ten apartments. One family went to the extreme of purchasing the empty space in front of their home in order not to have their view restricted. Despite the strict regulations which forbade Jews to leave the area from sunset to sunrise and prescribed the wearing of a yellow badge during daylight excursions, the Ghetto saw considerable incoming and outgoing traffic and became a vivacious social and cultural melting pot.

Though Shakespeare never mentions the Ghetto, the historian *Brian Pullan* has offered compelling evidence that seems to suggest that he had first-hand knowledge of local facts. For example, in 1589 two of the Christian gate-keepers of the Ghetto were "Gobbo" (like Shylock's servant in *The Merchant of Venice*) and his son; moreover both were involved in the Inquisition's trial of a Christian man, *Giorgio Moretto*, whose story is told in the chapter on the Carnival.

SHYLOCK – *Go, Tubal,*
and meet me at our synagogue. Go,
good Tubal; at our synagogue, Tubal.
[THE MERCHANT OF VENICE, Act III, Scene I]

 [31] "AT OUR SYNAGOGUE, TUBAL."

o which place of worship would Shylock have been referring when he arranges with Tubal to meet "at our synagogue"? The five main synagogues in the Ghetto (all are still in existence and visitable) were established in rapid succession to serve the various "nations" comprising the Jewish community there. Referred to in Venetian as *Scuola* and in Hebrew as *beth ha-kenesset* or meeting house, there are German, Italian, Levantine and Spanish synagogues and the *Scuola Canton*, which probably takes its name from a family or from its location (*canton* is Venetian for "corner").

Since only German Jews were allowed to lend money, Shylock would have attended the oldest of the synagogues, the *Scuola Grande Tedesca*, where the Ashkenazi rite was practised. Begun in 1529, the building is in the *Campo di Ghetto Nuovo* and can be identified from outside only by the windows overlooking the square, five like the books of the *Torah*.

The synagogue has a trapezoidal plan and set into the parallel sides are the *aron-ha-kodesh*, the sacred cabinet where the scrolls of the *Torah* were kept, and the pulpit or *bimà*. The oval women's gallery was added in the 1700s but the wooden panelling covering the lower parts of the walls of the main chamber, the *marmorino* plaster and the Ten Commandments in gilded Hebrew characters all date from the 1500s. Despite the absence of "graven images", forbidden by the Second Commandment, many decorative elements resemble the styles and materials found in churches because the synagogues were actually built and decorated by Christian craftsmen.

An alternative theory, proposed by the historian *Cecil Roth* in 1933, is that Shylock might have been a Spanish or a Portuguese Jew, or maybe even a *converso* or one of those ex-*marranos*, sometimes accused in Venice of lending money illegally at much higher rates of interest than those set officially. In this case, Shylock would have attended the impressive and richly decorated *Scuola Spagnola*, which stands in the *Campo di Ghetto Vecchio*. *Thomas Coryat* provides us with a valuable description of synagogue life at the beginning of the XVII century, a curious blend of admiration and criticism, interest and provocation, rooted prejudice and profound respect:

"*The Levite that readeth the law to them, hath before him at the time of divine service an exceeding long piece of parchment, rowled up upon two woodden handles: in which is written the whole summe and contents of Moyses law in Hebrew: that doth he (being discerned from the lay people onely by wearing of a redde cap, whereas the others doe weare redde hats) pronounce before the congregation not by a sober, distinct, and orderly reading, but by an exceeding loud yaling, undecent roaring, and Roaring not as it were a beastly bellowing of it forth [...] sometimes he cries out alone, and sometimes againe some others serving as it were his Clerkes hard without his seate, and within, do roare with him, but so that his voyce (which he straineth so high as if he sung for a wager) drowneth all the rest. One custome I observed amongst them very irreverent and prophane, that none*

The *Scuola Spagnola* is the biggest and most famous of the Venetian synagogues and the building is attributed to the school of *Baldassare Longhena*, the architect of the *Church of the Salute*. Recognizable by the fine wooden doorway and by the gilded Hebrew inscription on the arch, the synagogue was first built in 1580 but then re-structured in the mid-1600s with rich marble and wooden decorations that make it a small Baroque masterpiece. The attentive visitor will notice that one of the black slabs in the stone floor is out of place and disturbs the harmony of the pattern. The mistake is deliberate and is designed to remind us that we are imperfect beings: complete perfection is the prerogative of God. Or, as Shakespeare puts it in the *Rape of Lucrece*: "*no perfection is so absolute, / That some impurity doth not pollute.*"

of them, eyther when they enter the Synagogue, or when they sit downe in their places, or when they goe forth againe, doe any reverence or obeysance, answerable to such a place of the worship of God, eyther by uncovering their heads, kneeling, or any other externall gesture, but boldly dash into the roome with their Hebrew bookes in their handes, and presently sit in their places, without any more adoe; […] I observed some fewe of those Jewes especially some of the Levantines to bee such goodly and proper men, that then I said to my selfe our English proverbe: To looke like a Jewe (whereby is meant sometimes a weather beaten warp-faced fellow, sometimes a phrenticke and lunaticke person, sometimes one discontented) is not true. For indeed I noted some of them to be most elegant and sweet featured persons, which gave me occasion the more to lament their religion. […] In the roome wherin they celebrate their divine service, no women sit, but have a loft or gallery proper to them selves only, where I saw many Jewish women, whereof some were as beautiful as ever I saw, and so gorgeous in their apparel, jewels, chaines of gold, and rings adorned with precious stones, that some of our English Countesses do scarce exceede them."

However, any attempt to imagine Shylock as attached to one synagogue rather than another, to make him an *Ashkenazi* rather than a *Sephardi* Jew, or even to find biblical roots for his mysterious name (some have suggested links with *Shiloh*, a biblical term which Christians associate with the Messiah, or with the *Shelah* mentioned in Genesis) clashes with the evidence that Shylock was a purely English name, equivalent to Whitehead in its meaning of "with white hair". As in the case of Othello, Shakespeare certainly did not take the name from his Italian sources. Indeed, as *Stephen Orgel* has shown, by choosing the name Shylock, Shakespeare probably wanted to make fun of an English money-lender who belonged to the *Puritans*, the strict Protestants that loved to identify with the single-minded devotion of the ancient Hebrews of the Bible.

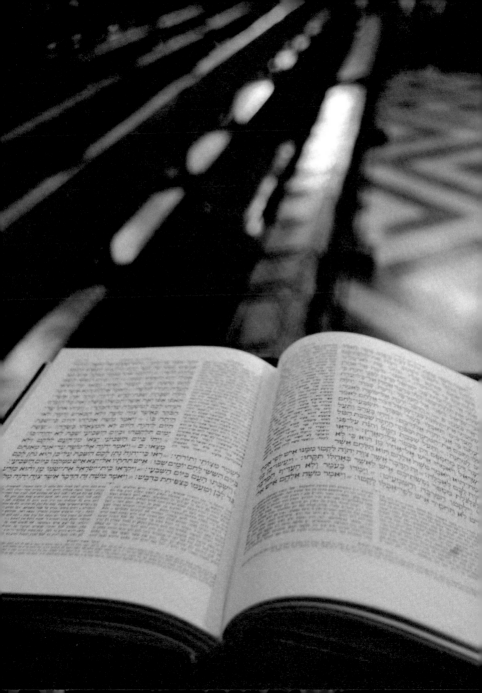

SHYLOCK – *Three thousand ducats for three months,*
and Antonio bound.
[THE MERCHANT OF VENICE, Act I, Scene III]

SHYLOCK – *He lends out money gratis and brings down*
The rate of usance here with us in Venice.
If I can catch him once upon the hip,
I will feed fat the ancient grudge I bear him.
He hates our sacred nation and he rails
Even there where merchants most do congregate
On me, my bargains, and my well-won thrift,
Which he calls interest.
[THE MERCHANT OF VENICE, Act I, Scene III]

 [32] A QUESTION OF "INTEREST"

n the *campo del Ghetto Nuovo*, under a portico and outside house number 2912, one can still see the sign marking the premises of the *Banco Rosso*, one of the pawn shops through which the Jews were able to carry on their money-lending service.
Like modern banks, these were financial operations that were allowed to make small loans against the deposit of some form of pledge or collateral. The charter of 1624, which restated rules established half a century earlier, authorized the German Jews (and only them) as follows: "*for the greater convenience of the poor, the Jews shall be bound to provide them with loans of 3 ducats or less in each pawn ticket, upon interest of 1 bagattino per lira per month and no more (=5 per cent per annum).*"
The historian *Brian Pullan* has shown how certain details of the story of *The Merchant of Venice* bear surprising resemblances to a series of events that actually took place in Venice in 1567. Though a Venetian Jew could not

lend more than three ducats and though in *Il Pecorone*, the novella by *Ser Giovanni Fiorentino* from which Shakespeare had taken the plot of his play, the loan that the anonymous Jew of Mestre makes to the Venetian Ansaldo amounted to ten thousand florins, three thousand ducats is precisely the sum at stake in a legal action involving a Christian and a Jew. In this case, however, it is the Jew, *Abraham Abencini*, who accused the Portuguese Christians *Gaspar* and *Giovanni Riebeira*, of usury: they had forced him to pay off a loan by buying a box of pearls for more than twice their market value, in effect charging interest of over 25% on the original loan. Abencini won the case and Pullan notes that the English comedy *The three ladies of London*, which *Robert Wilson* wrote in the 1580s, features the same scenario of a Jew tricked by a Christian over credit of 3000 ducats. Was it a coincidence, wonders Pullan, or a literary retelling of a story that in some way had reached London from Venice?

But the story doesn't finish there: some years later it was discovered that the two Ribeiras were in fact *Marranos*, i.e. Jews who only kept up a superficial show of being Christians. They had indeed attempted to make their circumstances less precarious by arranging for Gaspar's son Giovanni to marry a young Jewess from the Ghetto, *Alumbra de Luna*. Giovanni then died and Gaspar was arrested by the Holy Office for having re-embraced the Jewish religion. Another leading figure in the story was Violante, Gaspar's daughter, who had refused to go along with her father's plans for her to marry into the prominent Jewish family of the Abrabanels and had married a Christian nobleman from Vicenza, *Vincenzo Scroffa*, instead. The additional fact that Gaspar Ribeira dealt in precious stones leads Pullan to speculate that he might have been a model for Shylock and that the independent-minded Violante would make a perfect Jessica.

The Merchant of Venice throbs with centuries of bitter Christian resentment over Jewish usury, but the perceptive modern reader will note that all the human and sentimental relationships in the play seem to depend on money. When Portia enters the courtroom disguised as the lawyer Balthazar, for example, and asks "*Which is the merchant here? And which the Jew?*", perhaps this is Shakespeare's ironic way of intimating that there is in fact no difference between Shylock and Antonio and that the value system underpinning the play seems to ensure that love and friendship, pure and simple, untainted by some form of material interest, are not part of its world.

How much were three thousand ducats worth in the period when Shylock lent the sum to Antonio? It's difficult to say, now, just as it's hard to judge its purchasing power. More useful, perhaps, would be to compare a number of historical data, keeping in mind that the second half of the XVI century saw the highest rate of inflation that the *Serenissima* had ever known (this was certainly a primary cause of the failure of all the private *banchi*); so by the end of the century the daughters of the richest noble families brought dowries of as much as 20-25,000 ducats to their marriages (much of it in the form of increasingly valuable real estate), while a construction worker might earn no more than 80 ducats for a whole year's work.

First minted under *Giovanni Dandolo* in 1284, the *ducat* was made of 3.5 grams of the purest gold; three thousand ducats therefore corresponded to ten and a half kilograms of gold! Curiously, it was in the mid-1500s that the word ducato gave way to zecchino or sequin. Then, from a literary point of view, there is an extraordinary parallel between *The Merchant of Venice* and *Don Quixote*, by *Miguel De Cervantes* (who also comes into the chapter on slavery): it is three thousand ducats that the central character of an evidently biographical tale in the first volume (which tells of the *Battle of Lepanto*), inherits from his father before going to sea, in the same period as the Turks conquered Cyprus. From the Merchant to the Moor in a few lines …

SHYLOCK — *Mark what Jacob did:*
When Laban and himself were compromised
That all the eanlings which were streaked and pied
Should fall as Jacob's hire, the ewes, being rank,
In end of autumn turnèd to the rams,
And when the work of generation was
Between these woolly breeders in the act,
The skilful shepherd peeled me certain wands,
And in the doing of the deed of kind
He stuck them up before the fulsome ewes
Who, then conceiving, did in eaning time
Fall parti-coloured lambs; and those were Jacob's.
This was a way to thrive; and he was blest;
And thrift is blessing, if men steal it not.
[THE MERCHANT OF VENICE, Act I, Scene III]

SUFFOLK — *He is returned in his opinions, which*
Have satisfied the king for his divorce,
Together with all famous colleges,
Almost, in Christendom. Shortly, I believe,
His second marriage shall be published…
[ALL IS TRUE (HENRY VIII), Act III, Scene II]

 [33] **A LEARNED RABBI**

ith the emphasis placed on the economic activities of the Jews in *The Merchant of Venice* we may risk forgetting that the Ghetto was also an extremely important centre of scholarship and of the propagation of Jewish culture. Suffice to mention that a third of all Jewish books published in Europe up to the mid-1600s – over one thousand two

hundred volumes – were produced in Venice. Amongst the most important were the first printed Talmud, the monumental compilation of ancient Jewish law and tradition, the paging of which is still the same as that devised for the first edition by the Christian printer *Daniel Bomberg*. Paradoxically, Jews were forbidden to print books but they acted as consultants and proofreaders for Christian typographers of publications in Hebrew, until in 1553 two of the latter fell out and following reciprocal accusations of blasphemy the Council of Ten ordered the burning of all Jewish books in St. Mark's Square. Jewish culture in Venice also had an important influence over English history because it was here that *Henry VIII*'s emissaries came in search of learned religious opinions on the levirate and ways in which he might justify divorce from *Catherine of Aragon*, thus starting the process that led to the Act of Supremacy and the split from Rome.

One of the leading figures in Jewish cultural life in Venice was Rabbi *Leon Modena*, a scientist and theologian, a great preacher and author and autobiographer, whose *Life of Judah* vividly evokes the intellectual life of the Ghetto. Modena was a reference point for his community and far beyond it: he himself tells of the many Christian vistors who came to the Italian Synagogue to listen to his sermons, which therefore had to be delivered in Italian. The loss of two of his beloved sons (one died as the result of an alchemical experiment and another was murdered by a gang of delinquents) caused Modena profound distress and throughout his life he was obsessed with gambling; but he is also remembered as the author of the first work written in the vernacular by a Jew with the aim of acquainting Christian readers with Jewish customs. His *Historia de' Riti ebraici* was in fact commissioned by the English ambassador *Henry Wotton* and written for King *James I* while Shakespeare was still alive, though it wasn't actually published until 1637. It has also been suggested that Modena was the "*learned Jewish Rabbin that spake good Latin*" whom *Thomas Coryat* met in the Ghetto and whom he engaged in lively theological debate on the figure of Christ.

Leon Modena's ability to enter into dialogue with Christians, overcoming the barriers of the Ghetto, made him a very different personality from Shylock, who notoriously rejected any convivial contact with Antonio and his friends, except when he expediently accepted Bassanio's invitation to dinner and thus gave Jessica her opportunity to run away with Lorenzo. But his powerful command of language, his fondness for subtle puns and his erudite disquisition on the flocks of Laban and Jacob suggest at least some similarities with Rabbi Modena who, amongst other things, could write poetry that sounded alike and had approximately parallel meanings in Hebrew and Italian.

The *Midrash Leon Modena*, that is the room in which he taught his numerous pupils, can still be seen, not far from the Levantine Synagogue and on the same side of the campo del Ghetto Vecchio. He died in Venice in 1648, at the age of 77, and is buried in the movingly picturesque *Old Jewish Cemetery* on the Lido. Given that he managed to squander all his money and died in abject poverty, a slab of stone from an old balcony had to be used to mark his tomb.

It is carved with an epitaph that Modena himself is traditionally thought to have written: "*Words of the dead / Four ells of earth were acquired from on high, a possession for eternity for Judas Leone da Modena. Be merciful to him (O Lord) and give him peace. Died, Saturday 27 Adar, 5408.*"

A contemporary, friend and disciple of the Rabbi was the poetess and conversationalist *Sara Copio Sullam*. The literary salon that she hosted at the height of the Ghetto's period of greatest splendour (the first half of the XVII century) was much frequented, and not only by Jewish intellectuals. Blonde and beautiful, she was one of the most cultivated women of her time, an expert composer of music and verse, an authority on the Old Testament and on the history, traditions and religion of the Jewish people and with a scholarly interest in philosophy, theology, astrology and classical literature, *Sara Copio Sullam* had no need of translations to read works written in Spanish, Hebrew, Latin, French and, obviously, Italian.

ANTONIO — *So please my lord the Duke and all the court*
To quit the fine for one half of his goods,
I am content, so he will let me have
The other half in use, to render it
Upon his death unto the gentleman
That lately stole his daughter.
Two things provided more: that for this favour
He presently become a Christian;
The other, that he do record a gift
Here in the court of all he dies possessed
Unto his son, Lorenzo, and his daughter.
[THE MERCHANT OF VENICE, Act VI, Scene I]

OTHELLO — *Are we turned Turks? and to ourselves do that*
Which heaven hath forbid the Ottomites?
[OTHELLO, Act II, Scene III]

 [34] "TURNING TURK"... TO BECOME CHRISTIAN
onversion is a prominent theme in both Shakespeare's Venetian plays. Shylock the Jew is forced to become a Christian to escape the death penalty, and thus follows his daughter Jessica, who converts for love of Lorenzo. Othello is another convert, though the story never makes it clear what faith he professed before. Was he a pagan like Balthazar, the black African member of the Three Magi, who represents the universal dimension of the Christian Church? Or was he a Moslem, like the Ottomans he is engaged to fight beneath the Venetian lion (and from whom he seems continually to need to dissociate himself) and like *Leo Africanus* (see the chapter entitled "*Ciao, slaves and Slavs*") who eventually returned to Islam? The experiences of Shylock and Othello remind us that throughout

the Mediterranean area, and especially in Venice, conversions were common and took many different forms. The most numerous were probably Ottoman Moslems, who had come to Venice as merchants or slaves from as early as the XII century. But it was not until 1557 that a catechumenical institute (for those undergoing instruction prior to Christian baptism) was established conveniently near the Ghetto in the parish of San Marcuola (the odd Venetian amalgam of the names of *Saints Ermagora* and *Fortunato*). The premises were later moved to *Santi Apostoli* and finally to *San Gregorio*, adjacent to the *Church of the Salute*, where one still finds placenames incorporating the word *Catecumeni*.

Conversions were not always sincerely undertaken, however, and when Shylock leaves the stage in Act IV, muttering "*I am content*" with the decision of the court to oblige him to convert and to surrender half his estate, many imagine that he will remain a Jew in secret. Venice was much criticized for allowing many *conversos* expelled from Spain to return to Judaism and settle in the Ghetto. *Riccardo Calimani*'s *History of the Ghetto of Venice* tells the story of *Giuseppe Francoso*, a twenty-year-old Jew who confessed in 1548 that he had been baptized four times in as many cities in order to benefit from the gifts of money or new clothes that came the destitute young man's way every time he converted. Jacomo alias Aaron alias Giuseppe was sentenced to the galleys for twenty years, and then to permanent exile, for making mock of the sacrament. Although the *Serenissima* celebrated important conversions, like that of the son of the founder of the Ghetto, *Asher Meshullam*, with great pomp, the state never exerted excessive pressure on Jews to convert and the Inquisition concentrated more on Christians suspected of professing the Jewish religion in secret while living as Christians. An example of a Venetian place associated with conversion from Islam is *calle de le Turchette* (and the bridge of the same name) near the *Church of San Barnaba*. The name recalls an event that took place in 1428, when a number of young Ottoman female prisoners of war were held here, in a large house with barred windows, in order to give them instruction prior to conversion. In fact many Turks, whether for opportunistic reasons or for sincere belief, converted to Christianity when they became "guests" of the *Serenissima*. And when the future Doge *Sebastiano Venier* returned to Venice after the great victory of Lepanto with spoils of war that included an entire harem of a hundred concubines, many of them quickly underwent conversion and married Venetians.

But it mustn't be forgotten that although "turning turk", which in Venice as in England was a colloquial expression meaning any kind of abasement and especially of betrayal (*Hamlet*, for example, says "*if the rest of my fortunes turn Turk with me*", Act III Scene II), in actual fact there were many Christian converts to Islam, some of whom rose to high appointments, including that of Grand Vizir, in the Ottoman Empire.

During the XVI and XVII centuries there were many voluntary conversions: these "Christians of Allah" as they were known, joined up as simple Janissaries or became "career Turks", attracted by the opportunities offered by the Sublime Porte – undreamt-of in Europe – to progress steadily up the social ladder irrespective of one's origins or social class.

In Shakespeare's day famous converts to Islam included an Admiral "*Hassan*" of the Turkish fleet (also known as "*Sinan Cicala*" from his original name of *Scipione Cicala*, he was a regenade citizen of Messina – or perhaps Genoa – and raided and plundered the ports of Southern Italy) and *Giovanni Dionigi*

Galeni of Calabria (who took part in the *Battle of Lepanto* as an admiral of the Turkish fleet under the Arab name *Euldj Alì Pascià*; sometimes known a *Ulugh Alì* or *Alì the renegade*, he was astute enough to leave the scene of battle before the Turkish forces were defeated). Before them there was *Paolo Da Campo*, a pirate from Catania, who was captured by the Venetians and sentenced never to leave Venice; he pleaded to be allowed to join the Venetian fleet as a common sailor but abjured his vows of loyalty to Venice and passed over to the enemy.

As noted by *Daniel Vitkus*, the late-XVI early - XVII century being a period of readjustment of the balance of power between the Ottoman empire and Europe, Shakespeare and his contemporaries were profoundly affected by post-Reformation concerns that led to extensive literary (and also theatrical) treatment of the theme of Christian – Moslem conversion, with conversion to Christianity being presented in a positive light while apostasy, heresy and insincere conversion provided frequent negative scenarios, as did contemporary polemics concerning Protestants and Catholics who renounced one form of Christiantity in favour of another.

And finally, some scholars have suggested that Marranos, as the subjects of not always voluntary conversion from one monotheistic religion to another, one culture to another, ended up by devising a value system of their own and thus, unwittingly, became the precursors of modern individualism, though the primacy of the individual was not sanctioned until the French Revolution, two centuries later.

BRABANZIO – *Ay, to me. She is abused, stol'n from me and corrupted*
By spells and medicines bought of mountebanks.
For nature so preposterously to err,
Being not deficient, blind, or lame of sense,
Sans witchcraft could not.
[OTHELLO, Act I, Scene III]

OTHELLO – *That handkerchief*
Did an Egyptian to my mother give,
She was a charmer and could almost read
The thoughts of people. She told her, while she kept it
'Twould make her amiable and subdue my father
Entirely to her love; but if she lost it
Or made gift of it, my father's eye
Should hold her loathed and his spirits should hunt
After new fancies.
[…] 'Tis true, there's magic in the web of it.
A sibyl that had numbered in the world
The sun to course two hundred compasses,
In her prophetic fury sewed the work;
The worms were hallowed that did breed the silk,
And it was dyed in mummy, which the skilful
Conserved of maidens' hearts.
[OTHELLO, Act III, Scene IV]

 [35] MAGIC AND MOUNTEBANKS
hen he discovers that his daughter Desdemona has eloped with
Othello and married him in secret, Brabantio has no doubt that
the Moor must have "*practised on her with foul charms*" and that

he was therefore "*an abuser of the world, a practiser / of arts inhibited and out of warrant*". Venice was famous as a centre of magic and the occult, both essential components of Renaissance knowledge, whether the high philosophical research of cabbalists and alchemists or the petty tricks of sorcerers and mountebanks. Traces of this tradition are to be found in *Corte del Strologo*, in the parish of *San Marcuola*. The name of the courtyard may derive from the surname of a family who once lived there. But impressed in the stones of Venice and the names of its public thoroughfares are the strangest of stories and the most beguiling of legends, so it is just as probable that Corte del Strologo was in fact the home of a "*strologo*", in other words of a magician or a fortune-teller. Merchants trading with the East imported not only costly spices and magnificent cloths into the city: Venetian ships also brought esoteric knowledge and beliefs concerning astrology and magic, particularly in the 1500s; they were popular both with the common people, who were always ready to believe what any charlatan might swear was irrefutable truth, and amongst the nobles.

Sixteenth century chronicles reported widely the claims of *Francesco Barozzi*, a patrician who boasted of being able conjure up any spirit from the afterworld within a ring traced with the blood of a murdered man. He also declared that he had discovered a plant at Candia – he called it the "happy" herb – that could give wisdom to the greatest dullard in the world; and that he was privy to the secret of how to make coins he had just spent return to his purse. Another of his claims was that he could make himself invisible, but he evidently lost the knack the instant he was denounced and arrested for he ended up with a sentence of life imprisonment on 16th October 1587.

But superstition and the practice of magic were not so easy to eradicate: the city was full of silverware and jewels which were attached beliefs, often going back to Roman times, in their magical properties. They "*provided protection from poison and fire, guaranteed victory and love, made men wise and invisible, calmed tempests and infernos and cured illnesses*".

High-ranking Venetian women moved in a shimmer of pearls, diamonds, rubies, sapphires, agates, emeralds, beryls and topazes. A chronicler of the time, the Milanese nobleman *Pietro Casola*, notes that as he was passing through Venice on his long journey to the Holy Land in 1494 he saw twenty-five damsels "*each one more beautiful than the next*" who were wearing "*so many jewels in their hair, around their necks and on their hands that those present were of the opinion that the accumulated gold, precious stones and pearls were worth a hundred thousand ducats*".

The handkerchief that Othello gives Desdemona also had magical properties. But despite her father's accusations, Desdemona swears before the Doge that Othello had won her heart not by magic potions or spells but by his fascinating and moving stories; not by witchcraft but by the power of words, which in the Renaissance were considered to possess a nonetheless potent form of natural magic.

IAGO – *Tell me but this,*
Have you not sometimes seen a handkerchief
Spotted with strawberries in your wife's hand?
OTHELLO – *I gave her such a one, 'twas my first gift.*
[OTHELLO, Act III, Scene III]

☞ [36] MISTAKING MULBERRIES FOR STRAWBERRIES
n the chapter on Othello's house we mentioned the curious
XIX century theory that the figure of the Moor was in fact
based on that of the real historical nobleman *Cristoforo Moro*.
Another story accompanying this fanciful suggestion is connected with the
Church of San Giobbe (the fact that Job, along with several other figures
from the Old Testament, including Moses, Zacharias and Samuel, is raised
to sainthood and has a church dedicated to him, is a peculiarly Venetian
phenomenon) not far from the Ghetto. In 1378 *Giovanni Contarini* founded a hospice for paupers and shortly afterwards had a small Gothic church
built nearby. He dedicated this – now the *Contarini Chapel* – to *Saint Job*,
the patron saint of silk merchants.
Later, to ensure continuity for this charitable work, *Lucia Contarini*, the
daughter and only heir of Giovanni, put the *Minor Observant Franciscan
Friars* in charge of the enlarged hospice and church. In 1443, *St. Bernardine
of Siena* preached in the church. Bernardine was a friend of Cristoforo
Moro, a pious and devout man who was elected Doge in 1462 and who
restarted the work to enlarge the church. In 1471, the year of his death,
Moro bequeathed ten thousand ducats to the Franciscans to continue the
work. The curiosity concerns his tomb, which is decorated with a sculpted
image of a mulberry tree (moro in Italian). *Rawdon Brown*, whom we mentioned earlier in connection with another tomb, that of *Norfolk*, suggested
that Cinzio's Othello the Moor was inspired by the figure of Cristoforo

Moro and that the mulberries on the tomb had been transformed into the strawberries that adorn Desdemona's handkerchief.

The connection represents a considerable flight of fancy, though the mulberries carved on the tomb are in fact somewhat tapered and the casual observer might indeed mistake them for strawberries, but what the story illustrates above all is Brown's determination to find material evidence in Venice of a real connection with Shakespeare. The XIX century was also the period when great English actors such as *William Charles Macready* and *Henry Irving* studied Venice, its history, art and iconography to ensure that the Othello or the Shylock that they portrayed on stage were as "realistic" as possible, though such realism had nothing to do with Shakespeare and his times. Perhaps the surprising thing is that so many tourist and artistic guides to Venice continue uncritically to repeat anecdotes like that of the tomb at San Giobbe and take mulberries for strawberries.

Flourish of cornets. Enter the Prince of Morocco,
a tawny Moor all in white, and three or four followers
accordingly, with Portia, Nerissa, and their train.
[THE MERCHANT OF VENICE, Act II, Scene II]

 [37] STORIES OF MOORS AND CAMELS

e have already seen how many "Moors" there are in St. Mark's Square, and how different they are from each other. But there are other places with names associated with "Moors", the most charming without doubt being *campo dei Mori*, not far from the *Church of Madonna dell'Orto*.

Shakespeare and his contemporaries sometimes felt the need to distinguish between "Moors" of differing darkness of complexion: in *John Pory's* translation of the famous *History and Description of Africa* by *Leo Africanus* (a diplomat and great Moslem intellectual who, like Othello, was captured and became a slave), Shakespeare had probably read that: "*all the Negros or blacke Moores take their descent from Chus, the sonne of Cham, who was the sonne of Noe. But whatsoeuer difference there be betweene the Negros and tawnie Moores, certaine it is that they had all one beginning*". This reinforces the sensation that the term *Moor/moro* could have many different meanings, as we see again with the four *mori* (though accredited sources, despite the visible evidence, speak of three statues …) of this part of Venice.

Here there is a *palazzo*, the canal façade of which is decorated with the figure of a merchant with a camel, where the four *Mastelli brothers (Rioba, Sandi* and *Afani* and another whose name is lost) lived from 1112, when they fled to Venice to escape the disturbances in their native Greece.

They came originally from Morea, as the Peleponnese was then known, and so, however improperly, were known as *mori*, and their four statues became a landmark for Venetians. Indeed, their *palazzo* and the adjacent buildings came to be known as the *Fondaco degli arabi* (trading place and warehouse of the Arabs), although the Mastelli brothers took part in the 1202 Crusade led by Doge *Enrico Dandolo*. As regards the four highly distinctive statues, popular legend has it that everyone could recall an instance of rudeness, dishonesty or sharp practice suffered at the hands of Antonio Rioba or one of the merchant's three brothers; all four enjoyed their reputation as unscrupulous businessmen and it took them no time to ruin an unknown number of families and reduce hundreds of people to starvation and misery.

One evening there was a knock at the door of Ca' Mastelli. It was a woman who needed to buy material for her haberdasher's shop. Sensing a profitable deal, Rioba accompanied her personally to the warehouse, where his brothers were sorting their merchandise. «My husband died two months ago,» explained the woman, «and I have to re-open the shop at San Salvador. Good sirs, this is all the money left for me and my children to revive the fortunes of the shop and earn ourselves a living. So please, make sure we spend well and you will have gained a good and grateful customer».

Rioba couldn't believe his luck, practically having a whole shop in the centre of Venice being thrown into his lap like that. So, with a wink to his brothers, he set up the deal. «Look,» he said, showing the woman a couple of bolts of simple printed cotton, «I can hardly bring myself to part from this fine Flanders fabric, and indeed your money is nothing like enough, but I really do want to help you. Stock this cloth and you will have women fighting to get into the shop. And let God turn this hand of mine to stone if what I say is not true! Brothers, you come and swear too!». «I accept, good sir,» said the woman, placing her ducats in his hand, «and I call upon God to be witness to your honesty and to the commitment you have made.» Immediately the coins turned to stone, and with them the hand and arm of the man. And horror-struck, the other brothers saw their hands and arms transformed into stone. «You wicked, dishonest hypocrites. May you now become the whited sepulchres you have shown yourselves to be in life.» The woman was St. Mary Magdalene, who had made one last attempt to see if there was still some inkling of a chance of redemption. So the merchants were turned into the statues we see to this day, set into the outside walls of the house where they lived.

Irrespective of the origins of the Mastelli brothers, the statues undoubtedly depict people in oriental dress. In particular the turban, the shawl and the box held by one of the mori might suggest a Levantine Jewish merchant or more probably a Moslem *ulema* with his alms box.

As for the frieze with the camel, it too has inspired a folk tale, a romantic story that has more to do with the Orient of "A thousand and one nights" than nearby Greece. It tells of an Arab prince who lived in this palazzo, having decided to conduct his business affairs from Venice. Wishing to take a wife, he sent word to his betrothed, a young noblewoman of his country, to join him in Venice. Before leaving, she asked how she would recognize her loved one's *palazzo* amongst all those in the city. He answered that as soon as she passed in front of the building, she would have no doubt that it was the right one.

So she embarked on her long voyage and continued by gondola when she arrived in Venice. The gondola took her from canal to canal, hour after hour until finally, towards evening, it passed before *Ca' Mastelli*. A glance at the façade was enough to know that this was the right place and so the lovers were reunited.

OTHELLO – *Haply for I am black*
And have not those soft parts of conversation
That chamberers have.
[OTHELLO, Act III, Scene III]

 [38] **THE IRRESISTIBLE FASHION FOR BLACKAMOORS**
e have already looked at the various "Moors" that Shakespeare might have seen around Venice and we have mentioned the presence of black slaves in Venetian art. And although it dates mainly from periods later than Shakespeare's, we must also refer to the fashion for producing objects depicting Africans, always in a position of submission (and let's not forget that Othello is confident of his welcome in Venice as a result of the services he has rendered to the Serenissima).

In Venetian palazzi, in antique shops and in the workshops of wood-carvers and lacquerers one often sees "moretti", black servant figures holding candlesticks. Door handles and knockers frequently take the shape of African heads, their faces often seeming proudly to rebel against the strange form of imprisonment to which they seem destined. Most popular of all is probably the jewellery, especially the blackamoor head brooches with a white turban that are a traditional expression of the goldsmith's art in Venice.

Numerous legends claim to explain the origins of this unusual jewel. One of them goes back to the XVI century and tells of the terrible siege of the city

---

The contemporary American artist *Fred Wilson* was so fascinated by the African presence in Venetian Renaissance art that he created several fine post-modern works of art featuring some of the most famous examples, from *Carpaccio's* gondolier to the statues supporting *Doge Pesaro's tomb*. The exhibition in which he displayed this gallery of figures was called *"Speak of Me As I Am"*, the words pronounced by Othello as he is about to die.

of Fiume (Rijeka) in present-day Croatia. Terror reigned: for weeks the men had been manning the ramparts of the fortress repelling the increasingly ferocious attacks of the Saracens; now exhausted, they had given up hope of any form of relief but their womenfolk, barricaded inside the houses, still prayed constantly that their lives and the city might be saved. One day, an arrow shot by the nobleman Zrinski and guided by the hand of God struck the Turkish pasha in the temple. Seeing their commander fall dead, the Turks fled. But the heavens too opened in answer to the prayers of the women of Fiume and cast down such an avalanche of stones that all that could be seen of the buried Saracens were their white turbans. And to commemorate that victory, the men had "*moretti*" earrings made for all the women.

In Venice it was worn as an amulet to ward off attack from the sea and later came to represent a Turkish pirate reduced to slavery. Passers-by now regard them simply as curious ornamental objects but perhaps we ought rather to see them as dramatic figures trapped in decorative form and the compliant smiles of the be-turbaned "*moretti*" as concealing the sufferings that so many Africans were subjected to in the service of Venice.

OTHELLO – *Soft you, a word or two before you go.*
I have done the state some service, and they know't.
[OTHELLO, Act V, Scene II]

[…] *some forrain men and strangers haue been adopted into this number of cit-*
izens, eyther in regard of their great nobility, or that they had beene dutifull
towardes the state, or els had done vnto them some notable seruice
[G. Contarini, L. Lewkenor, *The Commonwealth and Gouernment of Venice*, London 1599]

 [39] **THE MYTH OF VENICE: GASPARO CONTARINI**
hough scholars are generally sceptical that Shakespeare ever
travelled abroad, they agree that his knowledge of the official history of Venice came from the English translation of
a very well-known and much read book that was published around the
same time as *The Merchant of Venice* and *Othello*.
This was *De magistratibus et republica venetorum libri quinque*, which the
Venetian Cardinal *Gasparo Contarini* published in Venice in 1551. Considered one of the key texts in the propaganda effort Venice made to
reinforce the symbolic power of the city at a time when its political power
was on the decline, the Latin original was translated into English "in his
free time" by the politician and courtier *Lewis Lewkenor* (he also incorporated extracts from other Venetian books, especially *Francesco*
Sansovino's Venetia città nobilissima et singolare of 1581) and published it
as *The Commonwealth and Gouernment of Venice*.
A clear indication of the fortune the book enjoyed in England occurs in
Volpone, the celebrated comedy that Shakespeare's contemporary and fellow
playwright *Ben Jonson* set in Venice and gives the character Sir Politick
Would-Be the line: "*I had read Contarine, took me a house*" [Act IV Scene I].
Scholars suggest that amongst the ways Contarini's book influenced

Shakespeare were the weight he placed on the presence of foreigners in Venice and his explanation of the military appointments that the *Serenissima* entrusted to non-Venetian professional soldiers (see also the chapter dedicated to *Bartolomeo Colleoni*). Possible echoes of the work may also be traceable in the epitaph that Othello gives himself ("*I have done the state some service, and they know't*") just before he takes his own life, or in Brabantio's mention of the "special officers of night", which recalls a passage in Lewkenor's translation: "*out of every tribe (for the city is divided into six tribes), there is elected an officer of the night [whose duty] is to keep a watch every night by turn, within their tribes*". The visitor to Venice can see a bust of Contarini in the *Church of the Madonna dell'Orto*, and the canal-side path that leads to the church is also named after him. His story is interwoven with that of the *Council of Trent*. During the period he was on state business in Germany he was one of the few to grasp the fact the Luther's rebellion was never going to be repressed by papal bulls or reprimands. On the contrary, Contarini saw clearly that what was needed was serious reform of the Roman Curia.

Gasparo Contarini (1483-1542) was made a cardinal by Pope *Paul III* in 1535, though the two had never met and Contarini was not even informed of the appointment (the same circumstances surrounded the promotion of *Giampietro* *Carafa*, who later became Pope *Paul IV*). Of noble birth, Contarini studied in Padua and then worked in an administrative capacity for the state; he eventually became Venetian Ambassador to the court of the powerful *Charles V* and later to the Vatican.

Perhaps this was why he was sent to Ratisbon in 1541 with a view to negotiating an agreement with the Reformists, but the meeting came to nothing because the parties were already so far apart that schism between the Catholics and the Protestants had become inevitable. In the Council of Trent, Contarini aligned himself with the more moderate wing, which was overwhelmed by events and he even had to defend himself against charges of heresy. He died in Bologna in 1542, where he had been sent as Papal Legate to enforce the decisions of the Council.

Apart from the more or less direct echoes of Contarini's book in Shakespeare, the English playwright seems not to have been taken in by the myth of Venice; he was much more interested in the reality of human relationships and in trying to convey what it really might have meant to be a foreigner, an outsider, in Venice.

BASSANIO – *So may the outward shows be least themselves.*
The world is still deceived with ornament.
In law, what plea so tainted and corrupt,
But being seasoned with a gracious voice,
Obscures the show of evil? In religion,
What damnèd error but some sober brow
Will bless it and approve it with a text,
Hiding the grossness with fair ornament?
[THE MERCHANT OF VENICE, Act III, Scene II]

KING HENRY – [Aside] *I may perceive*
These cardinals trifle with me: I abhor
This dilatory sloth and tricks of Rome.
[ALL IS TRUE (HENRY VIII), Act II, Scene IV]

 ☞ [40] OPPOSITION TO ROME: PAOLO SARPI

as Shakespeare a devout member of the Church of England, an incognito Catholic like his father or an atheist like his rival playwright *Christopher Marlowe*? In recent years there has been a lively debate as to the role of religion in Shakespeare's works and to what his personal feelings might have been at a time, moreover, when religion was an ever-present issue in political questions. It is, of course, extremely difficult to reach definite conclusions. First and foremost, Shakespeare was a man of the theatre and his plays give voice to dozens of different characters, but equally important was the fact that vigilant censorship forced him to become legendarily elusive.

Biographer *Stephen Greenblatt* writes of his *"astonishing capacity to be everywhere and nowhere, to assume all positions and to slip free of all constraints"*. But although attempts to make him out to be a card-carrying member of a particular political or religious group tend to be driven by a combination of pre-judged conclusions and wishful thinking, recent studies have turned up interesting evidence that Shakespeare was close to a group of intellectuals who, worried by the wars of religion that had torn France apart and were now threatening the rest of Europe, were trying to find a stable point of balance between religious and secular power. One of the leading thinkers of this movement was *Paolo Sarpi*, who wrote a *History of the Council of Trent* and was a supporter of Venice when the Pope placed the Republic under an interdict. Sarpi was born in 1552 and joined the Servite order at the age of 14. He was studious by nature and read widely not only in Latin and theology but also in philosophy, mathematics, Greek and Hebrew. At 27, Sarpi was appointed Provincial of his order and in 1606, as Consultor to the government of Venice, Sarpi defended the *Serenissima* in its dispute with the Church of Rome and argued that Pope *Paul V*'s interdict was invalid (the Pope had demanded that Venice repeal a law restricting church building and that two priests, whom the Republic intended to try before the civil court of the Council of Ten, should be handed over to him).

The Venetian Senate stood firm and declared that the Pope's infallibility extended only to matters of faith and that "princes have their authority from God and are accountable to none but Him for the government of their people". Publication of the papal bull was forbidden, all churches were ordered to celebrate mass and the religious orders that refused to obey were banned. With the support of Sarpi, Venice professed unfailing respect for the Catholic faith but asserted that deference to religious doctrine could not be in conflict with the laws of the State.

The interdict was lifted a year later on 22nd April 1607: Venice continued to pass laws concerning church property and to pass judgement on priests it found guilty and persisted in jealously asserting its rights with respect to the papacy, such as when it refused to recognize *Federico Corner* as Bishop of Padua and Cardinal because he was the son of the current Doge, or when it declined to use the new title of "Eminence" for cardinals.

But the Vatican did not take kindly to this diplomatic defeat and on the 5th October that year Paolo Sarpi was attacked and stabbed by five hired killers at the foot of the *Bridge of Santa Fosca*. The story of the attempted assassination is told by Brother *Fulgenzio Micanzio*, a follower of Sarpi: "*as the padre was returning to his monastery from St. Mark's he had just crossed the bridge at S.ta Fosca when he was attacked by five assassins, some of whom were acting as guards to the killers. The innocent padre received three stab wounds, two to the neck and one to the face, with the point of entry near the right ear and of exit between the nose and the right cheek; since the blade passed through bone the assassin was unable to withdraw the dagger and it remained embedded and twisted [...] At first the killer had plenty of time and he struck over fifteen times, as women at nearby windows witnessed and as was confirmed by the holes in his hat, in his hood and in the collar of his jacket, but he was wounded in only three places [...] The padre later had the dagger hung from the foot of a crucifix in the Church of the Servi [...] with the inscription:* DEI FILIO LIBERATORI* ".*

Sarpi survived the attack, though his injuries were serious, and from the first had no doubts about who was behind it: as the surgeon was extracting the dagger (*stilo*) from his face, Sarpi found the strength to make a punning comment on the fact that the wounds had been inflicted "*stilo Romanae curiae*". He died in 1623, having spent all his life in the Servite Monastery, which was demolished in the XIX century. A *statue of Paolo Sarpi*, one of the few erected to public figures in Venice, stands in *Campo Santa Fosca*.

APPENDIX

illiam Shakespeare, the eldest son of *John Shakespeare*, a successful glover and alderman, and *Mary Arden*, was born in Stratford-on-Avon, and baptised on 26 April 1564. He attended the local grammar school in Stratford, where he studied primarily Latin rhetoric, logic, and literature. At the age of 18 he married *Anne Hathaway*, a local farmer's daughter eight years his senior. The wedding was arranged in some haste because she was three months pregnant. Their first daughter, *Susanna*, was born six months later in 1583, and twins *Judith* and *Hamnet* were born in 1585. *Hamnet* died in 1596. After his marriage, Shakespeare left few traces in the historical record until he appeared on the London theatrical scene. The period from 1585 until 1592 is known as Shakespeare's "lost years" because no evidence has survived to show exactly where he was, although some scholars suggest that he worked as a country school teacher for Catholic families in Lancashire.

By 1592, Shakespeare was so well known in London that his fellow playwright Robert Greene called him "an upstart crow, beautified with our feathers". By late 1594, Shakespeare was an actor, writer and shareholder of a playing company known as the "Lord Chamberlain's Men" – named after their aristocratic patron. Their success was such that after the death of Elizabeth I in 1603 the new monarch James I adopted the company and they became known as the "King's Men".

In a career spanning twenty years, Shakespeare wrote and staged thirty-seven plays and some best selling poems, including his Sonnets (published without his consent). His masterpieces, besides the Venetian works, include his tragedies *Hamlet*, *Macbeth*, *King Lear* and *Romeo and Juliet*, his comedies *The Taming of the Shrew*, *Much Ado About Nothing* and *A Midsummer Night's Dream* and several history plays including *Henry V* and the two parts of *Henry IV*.

Shakespeare grew rich enough to buy property in London and own the second-largest house in Stratford, where he retired in 1613. He died there on 23 April 1616 and is buried in *Holy Trinity Church*. In 1623 *John Heminges* and *Henry Condell* published the first collected edition of his works, the so-called *First Folio*. Shakespeare is considered by many to be the greatest writer of all times.

THE
Tragœdy of Othello,

The Moore of Venice.

As it hath beene diuerse times acted at the
Globe, and at the Black Friers, by
his Maiesties Seruants.

Written by VVilliam Shakespeare.

LONDON,
Printed by *N. O.* for *Thomas Walkley,* and are to be sold at his
shop, at the Eagle and Child, in Brittans Bursse.
1 6 2 2.

THE TRAGEDY OF OTHELLO, THE MOOR OF VENICE

Shakespeare wrote *The Tragedy of Othello, the Moor of Venice* between 1602 and 1604, the year when it was presented at court. The play was published in 1622. The main source of the plot is the seventh novella of the third decade of *Gli Hecatommithi* (1565) by the Italian *Giambattista Giraldi Cinzio*.

THE PLOT

ate one night, *Iago*, the ensign or A.D.C. to *Othello*, a Moorish general in the service of Venice, tells *Roderigo* how *Othello* has promoted *Cassio* to become his lieutenant instead of *Iago* himself; he also reveals that *Othello* has secretly married the daughter of Senator *Brabantio*, *Desdemona*, with whom *Roderigo* is in love. The pair shout from the street to wake the Senator with the news that "*Even now, now, very now, an old black ram/Is tupping your white ewe*".

The *Doge* summons *Othello* urgently because the Turks are about to attack Cyprus. At the same time, *Brabantio* enters and accuses *Othello* of having used witchcraft to abduct his daughter. *Othello* presents an eloquent defence and *Desdemona* confirms that they are deeply in love. The *Doge* acquits *Othello* of any ill-doing (to the annoyance of *Brabantio*) and sends him to Cyprus.

The scene moves to Cyprus, where an unexpected storm has sunk the Turkish fleet and averted the battle. Observing the friendship between *Cassio* and *Desdemona*, *Iago* decides to set a trap, with the help of *Roderigo*. During the festivities to celebrate the victory and the general's marriage, *Iago* manages to get *Cassio* drunk and to involve him in a quarrel with *Roderigo* and *Montano*. *Othello* punishes *Cassio* with demotion and replaces him with *Iago*. In desperation, *Cassio* asks *Desdemona* to help him regain the general's favour. She intercedes for him.

Iago now begins to weave his web and gradually arouses suspicions in *Othello's* mind that his wife is being unfaithful; his warnings against jealousy only inflame *Othello's* unease and mistrust still further. Little by little, *Othello* is drawn into the trap and asks for concrete proof that the accusations are founded. When *Desdemona* accidentally drops a handkerchief given to her by *Othello*, *Iago's* wife, *Emilia*, passes it to her husband, who promptly informs *Othello* that he has seen it in *Cassio's* hands. Ingenuously confessing that she can no longer find the handkerchief, *Desdemona* continues to plead *Cassio's* case with *Othello*. *Cassio* now finds the handkerchief and asks the courtesan *Bianca* to make another just like it. Following a violent epileptic fit brought on by his growing anxiety at the suspicions being nurtured by the man he still believes to be his most trustworthy friend, *Othello* eavesdrops on a conversation between *Iago* and *Cassio*: they are in fact speaking of *Bianca* but *Othello* believes they are talking about *Desdemona*. When *Bianca* arrives with the copy of the handkerchief all doubts are dispelled: *Othello* has the proof he needs.

As *Lodovico* arrives from Venice with a letter from the *Doge*, *Othello* strikes *Desdemona* and, despite *Emilia's* insistence that she is perfectly innocent, insults and abuses her. Meanwhile *Iago* warns *Roderigo* that *Othello* and *Desdemona* are preparing to leave Cyprus and suggests that he get rid of *Cassio*, who is to take *Othello's* place.

Desdemona recalls the willow song, which her mother's maid used to sing her, a song that mourns the loss of love. *Roderigo* fails to kill *Cassio* and only manages to wound him on the leg. *Iago* comes to *Cassio's* aid and under cover of the scuffle disposes of *Roderigo*, whom he knows now wants to declare his love to *Desdemona*.

Now beside himself with jealousy, *Othello* smothers *Desdemona* in her bed, though she protests her innocence to the end. What *Emilia* discovers what has happened she tells *Othello* the truth about the handkerchief and *Iago* kills her. Realizing what a terrible mistake he has made, *Othello* stabs himself and dies beside *Desdemona*. *Iago* is dragged off to be tortured but refuses to explain the reasons for his treachery: "*What you know, you know*".

The moſt excellent

Hiſtorie of the *Merchant* of *Venice*.

VVith the extreame crueltie of *Shylocke* the Iewe
towards the ſayd Merchant, in cutting a iuſt pound
of his fleſh: and the obtayning of *Portia*
by the choyſe of three
cheſts.

As it hath beene diuers times acted by the Lord
Chamberlaine his Seruants.

Written by William Shakeſpeare.

AT LONDON,
Printed by *I. R.* for Thomas Heyes,
and are to be ſold in Paules Church-yard, at the
ſigne of the Greene Dragon.
1600.

THE MERCHANT OF VENICE

Shakespeare wrote *The Merchant of Venice* in 1596-97 and the play was published for the first time in 1600. His main source for the plot was an Italian novella in Ser Giovanni Fiorentino's collection *Il Pecorone* written in 1378 and re-published in 1558.

THE PLOT

 ntonio, a wealthy Venetian merchant, agrees to give financial help to his friend *Bassanio*, who needs to clear his debts if he is to present himself as a worthy suitor to the rich young heiress *Portia*, who lives at Belmont. *Antonio's* fortune is all tied up in maritime trade so he undertakes to arrange a loan. At Belmont, meanwhile, *Portia* bewails her fate to her maid *Nerissa*: her recently deceased father directed that she should not be allowed to choose a husband; the choice must be left to chance. She will marry the man who correctly identifies which of three caskets, made respectively of gold, silver and lead, contains her portrait.

Bassanio and *Antonio* ask the *Shylock* the Jew for a loan of three thousand ducats; he agrees, though he remembers how often *Antonio* has insulted him and his fellow-Jews at the Rialto. *Shylock* "in a merry sport" proposes a contract whereby failure to repay the debt at the appointed time and place will give *Shylock* the right to cut a pound of flesh from any part of *Antonio's* body. Despite *Bassanio's* protests, *Antonio* signs the bond.

[205]

The first suitor to approach *Portia*, the *Prince of Morocco*, arrives at Belmont. *Lancelot*, Shylock's servant, decides to run away from his master and places himself at the service of *Bassanio*. Shylock's beautiful daughter *Jessica* also wants to escape from what she feels to be prison-like circumstances and entrusts *Lancelot* with a letter addressed to her Christian lover *Lorenzo*, who has promised to marry her. Taking advantage of Shylock's absence (he has accepted Bassanio's invitation to dinner) *Jessica* dresses up as a man and leaves home, taking with her her father's gold and jewels.

At Belmont the *Prince of Morocco* chooses the gold casket and on opening it finds a skull instead of a portrait of Portia. Shylock reacts to the Jessica's flight with a mixture of desperation and rage. A second suitor, the *Prince of Aragon*, chooses the silver casket and discovers that it contains the portrait of an idiot. *Shylock* learns that Antonio's ships have all foundered and that *Jessica* is squandering his fortune. *Portia* has fallen in love with *Bassanio*, who has come to Belmont with his friend *Graziano*, and tries to dissuade him from attempting the test. But he is resolute and chooses the lead casket, where he finds the portrait of his beloved. *Portia* will marry *Bassanio* and *Graziano* will marry *Nerissa*, but *Lorenzo* and *Jessica* interrupt the joyful scene with the news that *Antonio* is ruined and that *Shylock*, furious at his daughter's flight, is determined to have his pound of flesh, which he intends to cut from near the heart. Bassanio returns to Venice to comfort his friend and shortly after, *Portia* and *Nerissa* decide to follow him disguised as men.

At the hearing, presided over by the *Doge*, *Shylock* demands payment as per contract and rejects all forms of alternative compensation. A young lawyer, *Balthasar*, and his assistant enter the court room: no-one knows that they are really *Portia* and *Nerissa* in disguise. *Shylock* once again refuses to entertain any appeal for mercy; he insists that case be judged according to the terms of the bond and Balthasar finds in his favour. But as *Shylock* prepares his knife, the lawyer points out that his rights are confined to taking a pound of flesh; if a drop of blood is shed he will be guilty of murder. At this point *Shylock* decides that he is prepared to accept money to settle the debt but it is too late: he is sentenced to give *Antonio* half his wealth and possessions, and the other half to the State. *Antonio* then proposes that the part due to the State be remitted, that the part due to him be held in trust for Jessica and that *Shylock* sign an undertaking to leave any wealth he has when he dies to *Jessica* and *Lorenzo*, to consent to his daughter's marriage and to convert to Christianity. *Shylock* leaves the stage muttering "I am content". *Balthasar* asks to be rewarded with the ring worn by *Bassanio* – a gift from *Portia*. *Bassanio* reluctantly agrees. Balthasar's assistant also persuades *Graziano* to part with the ring *Nerissa* gave him. When the two friends reach Belmont, *Portia* and *Nerissa* ask for an explanation as to why they no longer have the rings and then threaten to go to bed with the men to whom they have been given. *Antonio* intercedes and asks *Portia* to forgive *Bassanio*; she does so and gives him another ring – which turns out to be the one he gave *Balthasar*. The stratagem is now disclosed and all the couples can happily prepare for their weddings.

s often happens in the composition of a complex work, the writing of this book has benefited from the help, friendship and patience of many people who have given their contribution in different ways and at various times. The authors and the publisher wish especially to thank Olivia Alighiero, Matteo Casini, Susanne Franco, Giuseppe Gullino, Nancy Isenberg, Paola Modesti, Federico Moro, Reinhold Müller, Carol O'Brien, Gilberto Penzo, Enrique Perez de Guzman, Luca Pes, Luciano Pezzolo, Dorit Raines, Nick Robins, Valentina Spolaor, Patrick Spottiswoode, Laura Tosi, Alessandro Toso Fei, Micaela Vernassa and the Jewish community in Venice.

BIBLIOGRAPHY

SELECTED READING LIST

• All quotes from William Shakespeare, *The Complete Works*, eds. Stanley Wells and Gary Taylor, Oxford University Press, Oxford, 2005.

SHAKESPEARE'S LIFE AND WORKS

• Greenblatt, Stephen, *Will of the World. How Shakespeare Became Shakespeare*, Norton, New York, 2004.
• Shapiro, James, *1589. A year in the Life of Shakespeare*, Faber, London, 2005.
• Wells, Stanley, *Shakespeare: For All Time*, Oxford University Press, New York, 2002.

ON VENICE

• Chambers, David and Pullan, Brian, *Venice. A Documentary History 1450-1630*, Blackwell, Oxford, 1992.
• Coryat, Thomas, *Crudities* (1608), James MacLehose & Sons, Glasgow, 1905.
• Lane, Fredric, *Venice. A Maritime Republic*, The Johns Hopkins University Press, Baltimore, 1973.
• Lorenzetti, Giulio, *Venezia e il suo estuario*, Lint, Trieste, 1974.
• Norwich, John Julius, *A History of Venice*, Vintage, New York, 1989.
• Norwich, John Julius, *Paradise of Cities. Venice in the 19th Century*, Doubleday, New York, 2003.
• Ortalli Gherardo, Scarabello Giovanni, *A Short History of Venice*, Pacini, Pisa, 1999.
• Rosand, David, *The Myth of Venice. The figuration of a State*, University of North Carolina Press, Chapel Hill & London, 2001.
• Tassini, Giuseppe, *Curiosità veneziane*, Filippi, Venezia, 1988.
• Toso Fei, Alberto, *Veneziaenigma*, Elzeviro, Treviso, 2004.
• Toso Fei, Alberto, *Venetian Legends and Ghost Stories*, Elzeviro, Venezia, 2002.

SHAKESPEARE AND VENICE

• Brown, Horatio, *Studies in the History of Venice*, 2 vols, John Murray, London, 1907.
• McPherson, David C., *Shakespeare, Jonson, and the Myth of Venice*, University of Delaware Press, Newark, 1990.
• Marrapodi, Michele, *Shakespeare's Italy. The Function of Italian Locations in Renaissance Drama*, Manchester University Press, Manchester, 1993.
• *William Shakespeare and Italy*, edited by Holger Klein and Michele Marrapodi, Shakespeare Yearbook, X, 1999.
• Perosa, Sergio, *Shakespeare a Venezia*, Poligrafo, Venezia, 1991.
• Sacerdoti, Gilberto, *Sacrificio e sovranità. Teologia e politica nell'Europa di Shakespeare e Bruno*, Einaudi, Torino, 2002.

ON "THE MERCHANT OF VENICE"

- Gross, John, *Shylock. Four Hundred Years in the Life of a Legend*, Vintage, London, 1994.
- Calimani, *Riccardo, The Ghetto of Venice*, Evans and Co., New York, 1985.
- *The Jews of Early Modern Venice*, ed. by Robert Davis and Benjamin Ravid, Johns Hopkins Univ. Press, Baltimore, 2001.
- Orgel, Stephen, *Imagining Shakespeare. A History of Texts and Visions*, Palgrave Macmillan, London, 2003.
- Pullan, Brian, "Shakespeare's Shylock: Evidence from Venice" in *The Jews of Italy: Memory and Identity*, eds. Barnard Cooperman and Barbara Garvin, University Press of Maryland, Bethesda, 2000.
- Shapiro, James, *Shakespeare and the Jews*, Columbia University Press, New York, 1996
- Yates, Frances, *The Occult Philosophy in the Elizabethan Age*, London, 1979.

ON "OTELLO"

- Bassi, Shaul, *Le metamorfosi di Otello. Storia di un'etnicità immaginaria*, Bari, 2000.
- Phillips, Caryl, *The Nature of Blood*, Faber, London, 1997.
- Rosenberg, Marvin, *The Masks of Othello: The Search for the Identity of Othello, Iago, and Desdemona by Three Centuries of Actors and Critics*, University of California Press, Berkeley 1961.
- Serpieri, Alessandro, *Otello: l'Eros negato*, Liguori, Napoli, 2003.
- Vaughan, Virginia Mason, *Othello. A Contextual History*, Cambridge University Press, Cambridge, 1994.

SOURCES

- Brown, Horatio, *Studies in the History of Venice*, 2 vols, John Murray, London, 1907. [6]
- Bullough, Geoffrey, *Narrative and Dramatic Sources of Shakespeare*, London, Routledge & Kegan Paul, 1958. [7]
- Bodin, Jean, *Colloquium of the Seven about secrets of the sublime*, by Marion Leathers Daniels Kuntz, Princeton University Press, Princeton, 1975. [18]
- Calimani, Riccardo, *The Ghetto of Venice*, Evans and co., New York, 1985. [34]
- Cinzio, Giambattista Giraldi, *Gli Hecatommithi in Novelle del Cinquecento*, eds. G. Salinari, UTET, Torino, 1976. [9]
- Contarini, Gasparo, *De magistratibus et republica venetorum libri quinque*, Apud Baldum Sabinum, Venezia, 1551; trans. by Lewis Lewkenor, *The Commonwealth and Gouernment of Venice* (1599), Theatrum Orbis Terrarum, Amsterdam, 1969.[10, 39]
- Contarini Pietro, "Argo vulgar", Venezia, 1542, in *Venice: a Documentary History, 1450-1630*, Chambers, David and Pullan, Brian, Blackwell, Oxford, 1992. [1]

• Coryat, Thomas, *Crudities* (1608), James MacLehose & Sons, Glasgow, 1905. [1, 5, 7, 20, 28, 29, 31, 33]

• Gentili, Augusto, *Le storie di Carpaccio: Venezia, i Turchi, gli Ebrei*, Marsilio, Venezia, 1996. [11]

• Davis, Robert C, "Slave Redemption in Venice, 1585–1797", in *Venice Reconsidered: The History and Civilization of an Italian City-State, 1297-1797*, eds. Martin, John-Dennis Romano, Johns Hopkins, Baltimore, 2000, pp. 454-87. [26]

• Doody, Margaret Ann, *Tropic of Venice*, University of Pennsylvania Press, Philadelphia, 2006. [8]

• Empson, William, *The Structure of Complex Words*, Chatto and Windus, London, 1969. [25]

• Empson, William, *Essays on Renaissance Literature, Vol. 2: The Drama*, Cambridge Univ. Press, Cambridge, 1994. [12]

• Franco, Veronica, *Poems and selected letters*, edited and translated by Ann Rosalind Jones and Margaret F. Rosenthal, Chicago & London, The University of Chicago press, Chicago 1998. [23]

• Gleason, Elizabeth G., *Gasparo Contarini. Venice, Rome and Reform*, Univ. of California Press, Berkeley, 1993. [39]

• Greenblatt, Stephen, *Will in the World: How Shakespeare Became Shakespeare* W.W. Norton & Co., New York, 2004. [40]

• Honigmann, E.A.J. (ed.), *Othello* (Arden 3), Thomas Nelson and Sons, Walton-on-Thames, 1997. [8]

• Howells, William Dean, Howells, *Venetian Life* (1885), The Marlboro Press, Marlboro, Vermont, 1986. [30]

• Leo Africanus, *The History and Description of Africa*, trans. John Pory, London, 1600. [26, 37]

• Modena, Leone, *The autobiography of a Seventeenth-Century Venetian Rabbi : Leon Modena's Life of Judah*, Princeton University press, Princeton, 1988. [33]

• Norwich, John Julius, *Paradise of Cities.Venice in the 19th Century*, Doubleday, New York, 2003. [6]

• Orgel, Stephen, *Imagining Shakespeare. A History of Texts and Visions*, Palgrave Macmillan, London, 2003. [31]

• Partridge, Eric, *Shakespeare's Bawdy*, Routledge, London, 2001. [22]

• Pedani, Maria Pia, "*Venezia tra mori, turchi e persiani*", Vicenza, 2005, (http://venus.unive.it/mpedani/materiali.htm). [24]

• Pemble, John, *Venice Rediscovered*, Clarendon Press, Oxford, 1995. [16]

• Penzo, Gilberto, Navi veneziane: catalogo illustrato dei piani di costruzione = Venetian Ships : an Illustrated Catalogue of Draughts, LINT, Trieste 2000. [13]

• Phyllips, Caryl, The Nature of Blood, London, Faber, 1997. [5, 27]

• Preto, Paolo, I servizi segreti di Venezia, Milano, Il Saggiatore, 1994. [2]

• Pullan, Brian, "Lo 'Shylock di Shakespeare'; La testimonianza degli archivi di Venezia", in *L'identità dissimulata. Giudaizzanti iberici nell'Europa cristiana dell'età moderna*, ed. by Pier Cesare Ioly Zorattini, pp. 297-310, Olschki, Firenze, 2000. [34]

• Pullan, Brian, "Shakespeare's Shylock: Evidence from Venice" in *The Jews of Italy: Memory and Identity*, eds. Barnard Cooperman and Barbara Garvin, University Press of Maryland, Bethesda, 2000.

• Rosand, David, *Myths of Venice: the Figuration of a State*, The Univ. of North Carolina Press, Chapel Hill, 2001. [8]

• Roth, Cecil, *History of the Jews in Venice*, Schocken Books, New York, 1975. [31]

• Sacerdoti, Gilberto, *Nuovo cielo, nuova terra. La rivelazione copernicana di 'Antonio e Cleopatra' di Shakespeare*, Il Mulino, Bologna, 1990. [19]

• Sacerdoti, Gilberto, *Sacrificio e sovranità. Teologia e politica nell'Europa di Shakespeare e Bruno*, Einaudi, Torino, 2002. [18]

• Shapiro, James, *1599. A year in the Life of Shakespeare*, Faber, London, 2005. [11]

• Thomas, William, *History of Italy* (1549), Cornell University Press, Ithaca, 1963. [4, 24]

• Yates, Frances, *Astraea: The Imperial Theme In The Sixteenth Century*, Routledge and Kegan Paul, London, 1975. [1]

• Yates, Frances, *The Occult Philosophy in the Elizabethan Age*, Routledge & Kegan Paul, London, 1979. [12]

• Wilson, Fred, *Speak of Me As I Am*, MIT List Visual Arts Center, Boston 2003. [38]

• Wyatt, Michael, *Italian Encounter with Tudor England: a Cultural Politics of Translation*, Cambridge University Press, Cambridge, 2005 [21]

• Wynne Orsini Rosenberg, Giustiniana, *Du sejour des comtes du Nord à Venise en janvier MDCCLXXXII. Lettre de M.me la comtesse douairiere des Ursins, et Rosenberg à M.r Richard Wynne, son frere, à Londres*, Venezia, 1782. [17]

INDEX OF NAMES AND PLACES